Seeing The Incredible Aura

OTHER BOOKS BY THIS AUTHOR:

The Aura Coloring Book
Liberating Your Passionate Soul
Six Steps To A Better Life
Eco-Spirit, A Spiritual Guide to Healing The Planet
My Secret Clairvoyant Life
Healing Magick

BOOKS PUBLISHED IN TOKYO IN JAPANESE:

Give Yourself The Kind of Life You Have Always
Wanted To Have
Healing Practice I
Healing Practice II
Healing Practice III
Liberating Your Passionate Soul
Six Steps To A Better Life

Seeing The Incredible Aura

Your Stepping Stone to Enlightenment

Levanah Shell Bdolak

authorHOUSE®

AuthorHouse™
1663 Liberty Drive
Bloomington, IN 47403
www.authorhouse.com
Phone: 1-800-839-8640

First published by AuthorHouse   6/24/2009

ISBN: 978-1-4389-7783-6 (sc)

Printed in the United States of America
Bloomington, Indiana

This book is printed on acid-free paper.

Cover Art by
Inside Graphics

DEDICATION

I would like to dedicate this book to Mr. Taketoshi Hayashi, Mr. M. Nagai, Daiki Miyazawa and Sayaka Kunishige, Satchiko Shinkai, the Clearsight Clairvoyant Japan staff; and Maki Hatekayama & Yumi Kanno, the office staff of Clearsight Japan who has given me the support to be able to write this book.

I would also like to thank my Japanese interpreters, Hiroko Takahashi, Kaori Uenoyama, Rika Sekiguchi and Yumiko Hirose for their great help and aid in communicating clairvoyant skills to our students and their response back to me.

TABLE OF CONTENTS

INTRODUCTION

Seeing the aura can open you to an incredible world of awareness that can totally change your life. It can show you how to understand and know yourself as well as understanding your friends, family and business companions. Seeing the aura can show you how to recognize and heal disease before it manifests in the body. Viewing the life force energy around a person can open you to the true knowledge of human nature. You can learn to view the past, the present and the future. You can also learn to create the future you wish to have. But most of all, seeing the aura is the first stepping stone to enlightenment. It enables you to comprehend the energy universe and all that it encompasses.

You are born with the ability to see an aura. All I am doing in this book is reminding you that you have that ability within you. You are the same spirit as when you were born and the same spirit as before you were born. You are intrinsically empowered with your true nature, which is the spiritual nature of pure energy. Once you can acknowledge and allow this you will be on the road to your true path in this life. You will have empowered yourself to acknowledge your true divine nature. This divine nature is the true you that will give you a good life, and show you how to also help to create the "good life" for all in our physical world.

You are the best you can be if you act on it. The true inner you has the power to know all and the power to help to change the world in a better way. And to know this and to use this all you really have to do is to get to know your energy and connect with your Higher Self. One of the easiest and best ways to do this is to learn to see the aura.

Your aura is your life force. It is the reflection of who you are and who you can be.

I am writing this book in the hope of dispelling myths about the aura and inviting you to enter into the world of active spirit while living in your body. As you change yourself you will also change the world around you.

Studying the aura is not an esoteric past time. If you wish to be successful in life, to understand human nature in a deep manner and to fill your life with beauty and wonderment then you will want to learn to focus on seeing the aura.

Chapter One
Your Spirit In Action

Energy into Action

Are you happy? Are you getting what you want and need in life? Do you worry a great deal about your finances, your family, your health or your general well being? Do you take action when you think of a way to change your life? Or do you hesitate? Do your fears or your inspirations control you?

We have been taught in the modern world that it is our thoughts that control us. But I have learned that it is truly your energy that controls what you do and what you get in life. If you change your energy you can change your life. As you change your life it also changes your thoughts!

Most people live in a quagmire of fears and dreams. When they fear they cannot make their dreams come true then they sink into despair or what the modern pharmaceutical companies call depression. Depression is being unable to see a reason or purpose for your life. As a spiritual Being and a physical body personality you have life force energy that was built into your system to give you purpose in life. The problem occurs when people lose touch with how to make the connection with this life force energy. Then they look to others to tell them what is right and wrong, what is good or bad and what to do. They look to books, religious texts, and psychological explanations to enable them to know what to do and how to act.

The true book of life is within you. It is built into every gene in your body and all of your consciousness. You are a walking example of what people call the God force or the force of ONE. All that you could ever need to know how to live a happy loving inspired life is within you. And all you have to do is learn how to connect with that energy to live a truly fulfilling life. One of the first steps in connecting with your inner energy is to learn to see and know your aura. Your aura is the energy that surrounds your body. It protects you and displays to the outer world who your true self is. It also holds the energy of who you are within yourself---the "you" that is energy, a spiritual being in a physical form.

You are a colorful loving human being.

The aura is your soul's expression of who you are in action through this current living body.

As you learn to see your aura you learn to know your true self, the inner you that makes your decisions in life and knows your chosen destiny and how to create a loving abundant and energized life. To know the aura it helps to understand the energy machine within you that creates your aura. Once you understand your energy machinery and how it works you are capable of creating the life you want to have, a life filled with love, abundance, joy and good health. You are the creator of your life and your reality if you choose to use energy skills to make the reality you wish to have. With energy you can create the good life. Clairvoyant skills open the doorway to using your true inner abilities. Anyone can do this. You are born with this ability and just have to remind your energy self how to do this consciously.

YOUR ENERGY MACHINERY

There are many myths and much misinformation about what an aura is and how you can see it. I have had people tell me you have to have a person stand in front of a white wall to see their aura. This is not true at all. The aura can be seen at any time, in a lighted or a dark room, no matter where the person is standing or what he is standing in front of.

Last week I met a nice very intelligent woman who asked me what type of work I do in life. I explained to her that I show people skills to improve their life, get in touch with their energy self and I used the system of reading the aura to do this. She told me she had heard about seeing auras. She went on to explain to me that she had heard that if you squint your eyes and pull your eyes up so you are looking upwards over your head and then stare at the person whose aura you want to see, then you will see his aura. She also added that it would help if that person was standing in front of a white or bluish white wall. I was shocked by what she said. Everything she had been told was misinformation and not true at all. So many people have such confusion about seeing an aura or using their energy to create their own personal universe.

You are seeing the aura, not with your eyes, but with your inner eye, or what we clairvoyants call your sixth chakra.

A chakra is an energy center. The word chakra is a Sanskrit word and it has many meanings in Sanskrit. To simplify it a chakra is an energy center. It is shaped like a vortex that goes through your body with the wide part in the front and the narrow cone part in the back of you. A chakra is a part of your energy machinery. The sixth chakra is located in the center of your forehead and its function is to enable you to have vision in life so you can connect with your spiritual essence and see your path clearly.

Your sixth chakra opens and closes like a spiral, like the lens of a camera or the iris of an eye. Within your sixth chakra there is the machinery for seeing which is an energy projector that sends images of what you perceive onto a screen that is about a foot in front of your forehead. When you see something clairvoyantly you are actually viewing it on this screen. Many natural clairvoyants will tell you that they see pictures in their head. They are actually seeing these pictures on their screen but they do not realize this because when the picture is lit up on the screen you do not notice the screen. You just see the picture. (This is similar to when you go to the movies. Once the movie starts you do not notice the screen because you are watching the movie that is displayed on it!)

The sixth chakra energy projector and the screen are considered part of the sixth chakra machinery. The sixth chakra also has the ability to focus quite like the telephoto lens of a camera that can zoom in or out to see an image more clearly. Therefore you can choose to look at anything you wish to see. You can see the energy or colors in the back of your aura, or the aura of someone in another city. You just have to consciously choose what to look at.

We call the sixth chakra the "sixth" chakra because if you start at the First Chakra at the base of the spine and count upwards, the sixth one is located in your forehead. This is the Western method of labeling the chakras.

To learn more about the chakras, to read an explanation of the seven major chakras along your spine please refer to the Appendix of this book.

There are so many myths about seeing the aura. Some people sell aura viewing glasses and tell you that by using these you can see the aura. I have no idea if these really work. However, you do not need these aura viewing glasses some companies sell. You already have the ability to see an aura with your inner sight. Glasses do not improve or shift you to your inner sight. Your choice of consciousness is what shifts you to allow you to see an aura. Once you choose to use your inner consciousness to see an aura you can also learn to use your inner consciousness to change yourself and create the destiny you want in this life.

There is a myth that only special people can see the aura. This also is not true. You are a spiritual Being in a human body. All spiritual beings can see an aura. Of course, every time we reincarnate in a body we forget our past lives and seem to start all over again. So often we also lose touch with our spiritual nature and do not realize what skills, abilities and knowledge we have within ourselves. All people who want to can see an aura. You do not have to be special or highly evolved. You simply have to learn to clear yourself, to focus your energy and to give yourself permission. Most people do not know how to do this and so we have developed classes to show people the simple methods for releasing the energy that blocks you from seeing and how to learn to focus your energy fully. The interesting thing we have discovered from giving these classes is that when people clear themselves of old emotions and patterns and learn to focus their energy they also become more successful as well as being able to see auras.

Many little children under the age of eight see auras naturally. If you have a child under the age of eight at home see if you can ask him to tell you what color your aura is. You have to ask without bias in a very natural way. Once children turn eight they tend to want to be more social and more athletic. They start to put their attention on friends, games and activities outside of themselves and they stop looking at auras or speaking about spiritual matters. A few years ago I had a student in California who had a seven year old son. She was fascinated by what he would say to her. He recounted his past lives in detail, described his grandmother who had died when he was only two years old and sometimes told her the colors in her aura. She marveled at it and found it fascinating but always treated him as if this was all normal. When he turned eight he started playing baseball and stopped speaking about his past lives and his spiritual perceptions. She came to me and was devastated that he no longer seemed to care about spiritual matters. I explained to her that this was normal for a child, as now he had to reach out and encompass the world outside of himself. And I also explained to her that probably some day he would come to a class and say he would like to see auras but had never seen them. And then, after a few months of doing energy skills, he would most likely remember his spiritual childhood and easily see auras again. We have already had this happen to our students who take Clairvoyant classes. Seeing auras is a natural ability built into the energy skills of every living human being.

LIVING AS SPIRIT

You are a spiritual being in a physical body. Your spirit is what motivates your body to take action. You are alive because you literally have "spirit." Your spirit, or what we like to call your Higher Self, is the life giving part of you. It is your spirit that can heal you. It is your spirit that knows what is right and what works for the best in your life. It is your spirit that is the true you.

If you learn to walk as one with your spirit you become integrated with your higher nature. You become as a human god upon the earth. You become as one with the oneness. You become more than you are as a simple human and you become all that you are as being in touch with the divine on a constant level. You come to know life as a fullness that fills your body, your mind and your actions. You discover the true key to love and life and being alive in the most deepest manner. You become the living spirit. This is what all humans are meant to be. It is living up to your true potential. And it is connecting with all that is and leads you to a higher plane of awareness and the path to human evolution.

Living as spirit is your birthright and it is your fullest potential. It is what some spiritual traditions call enlightenment. However do not be fooled by the shallow concept of enlightenment. There is not one simple enlightenment but many levels of spiritual unfolding that eventually lead you to a higher and deeper level of awareness. The steps to heaven are many as the spirit keeps evolving. The human condition is one of the lowest levels until you release fear and emotions and turn to the light and embrace your Higher Self and its knowledge of the oneness. Then you live as spirit, which is what you were always meant to do. Walking this path can be a gradual learning curve although sometimes you will evolve faster as you have glimpses or revelations of your true self. Walking as spirit is walking with your divine self within you and being consciously aware. Walking as spirit is also called being consciously aware and awake.

SEEING AS SPIRIT

You do not see an aura with your eyes. You see an aura with your inner self, with your spirit. Your spirit, or what we call your Higher Self, can look and see anything---your past lives, your future lives, your aura, your friend's aura, when a storm is coming, what will happen in the next election, --world and personal events to come. You have to learn to focus and to communicate with your Higher Self in order to get your Higher Self to communicate these insights to you in a way you can comprehend, understand and use in your life.

Learning to focus your energy is not just learning to see an aura! If you read all of the best selling how to be successful in business books on the market these days you will soon realize that learning to focus and keep your focus is one of the prime tools used by the most successful business entrepreneurs.

HOW COLOR SPEAKS TO US AND WHAT IT SAYS

Color is the language of the body and the soul. Without realizing it you are constantly affected by the colors around you. Nowadays hospitals paint the walls of their waiting rooms green in order to create a calmness. Many restaurants paint their walls red so that their clients feel energized and so eat fast. Men in politics know to wear power ties—colors arranged to draw an essence of authority and power.

There are schools that can teach you what colors enhance your skin and show you to your best. Color coordinators can choose the right color dress or shirt for your skin color based on defining what seasonal color you belong to.

However, the colors of your aura are not superficial colors that make you look handsome or pretty, calm or energized, or powerful and charismatic. The colors of your aura are the colors of your soul. These colors tell what you are feeling inside. Colors of the aura reflect your feelings, your actions, your beliefs and your health.

LIFE IS FUN WHEN YOU CAN SEE AURAS

Since I have learned to see and view auras I have never had so much fun in my life. While others stand on line at the bank and the supermarket, being bored, stressed or just biding their time I look at the marvelous colors of people's auras who are also standing on line. I do not see just color but see into the inner soul of the people who stand around me. It is a journey of enlightenment and fun to just stand on line at the supermarket. Certainly you will never be bored if you can see auras! It is fascinating and is also an education as you learn from what you view!

CHAPTER TWO
INNER SIGHT

You cannot see an aura with your eyes. You see an aura with your inner eye, the energy center that is your sixth chakra. Your sixth chakra is the energy center located in the middle of your forehead. Chakra is a Sanskrit word. It has many definitions but the most common explanations are a wheel that spins or energy machinery. The sixth chakra has what we call the energy machinery---kind of like a camera--- to allow you to see pure energy. This energy machinery is built into every human being. It is a telescopic lens that focuses the images on a screen that is located about a foot in front of the middle of your forehead.

So essentially, clairvoyancy is simply the act of watching the movie of life on your screen. Often people ask me if this is real or is it simply seeing something in "your imagination."

Clairvoyants tend to call the imagination the ability to see in your mind's eye. You are not imagining something as in the act of "making up something that is not real." You are seeing living vivid pictures in color that are in your mind's eye. The pictures are real. They hold a tremendous amount of information that you can use to improve your life, your society and the planet if you wish to do so.

Clairvoyant information is different from the way we regularly pull in information, which is basically with our analytical mind. When you are using clairvoyancy you are seeing with your spiritual self. Your spiritual self is what is more commonly known as your Higher Self. This is the part of you that is the "true you."

Your Higher Self is you as an energy Being. It is your original essence, which is the part of you that hived off from the oneness and then started taking lives. Each time you incarnate in a body you learn many lessons and work your way back to the oneness we all came from.

When you see clairvoyantly you are seeing with the eyes of your soul, with the eyes of your Higher Self. Your Higher Self has a direct connection to the oneness or what we call the God Source. So your Higher Self can see anything it chooses to view. If you learn to connect with your Higher Self then you can see as your "spirit" sees. Then it is easy to see the aura or any type of energy.

Every living entity has an aura or what you might call a sphere of life force that surrounds it. All objects, animate or inanimate are created from energy. So all objects have energy.   But living objects have what we call "life force energy" and these are the energy centers within a living being and the aura that surrounds it.

Your aura holds the information of who you are and what you are doing now. Your aura also protects you. It is your personal universe. Whatever is within your aura is what you will create within your current world. This is why clairvoyants learn to clear the aura to release old patterns programs and emotions. If you let go of the way you did things in the past you will create a new future for yourself.

Using your inner sight is using your ability to see colors, pictures (images) and energy centers (chakras). Your inner sight gives you the knowledge of the true essence of a person.

So what does inner sight teach or show you that you cannot see with the normal naked human eye?

Inner sight teaches insight to see what you feel inside and *why* you feel it. Inner sight teaches you why certain incidents happen in your life. Nothing happens due to coincidence. Each experience in life is there to teach or show you something.

I had a student who was in four car accidents. She did not get hurt. But in each accident someone in a car came along and hit her---always from behind. She came to me and asked me to look clairvoyantly to see why this was happening to her. It was obvious that in her life she was sitting still and not moving on any of her goals. She was afraid to change. She was afraid to shift into a new part of her life. So her Higher Self finally decided to allow other cars to hit her from behind to show her she needed to push herself to move in life. She would see the car behind her moving too fast towards her but she would freeze and not move her car out of the way. Her lesson was to move in her life. Her Higher Self had tried to communicate this to her in many ways but she would not listen to get the message. So finally her Higher Self decides to make it extreme enough for her to wake up and take notice, to listen and to ask why these accidents were happening to her. After she understood she began to allow herself to take action in her life and the accidents stopped happening.

Everything happens for a reason. Sometimes the things that happen are very small and we do not notice or consider them til much later in life when we see the pattern in retrospect. Looking back at what happened is always a much easier way to see and understand your patterns and life issues. But learning to read clairvoyantly is learning to see these things right in the moment when they are happening so that you can shift your life immediately. It empowers you so that you can create the quality type of life you really want to have.

Inner sight allows you to know why you meet someone, your past life patterns with that person, your connection and what you need to learn from one another. Inner sight shows you the true meaning in your life, what you came here to do in this life and how to do it. This allows you to directly communicate with your divine nature and so to evolve to a higher level of your potential.

Accessing your Inner Level of Awareness

Your inner level of awareness is not just how you feel emotionally or how your body feels. Within you is the energy that truly creates who you are and what you do. Let me give you an example. In many ways it is your emotional feelings that drive what you do. I have a friend who keeps a large bowl of bite size bars of candy on his desk. While I was visiting he explained to his wife and I how he had decided to go on a diet and to quit eating candy. About a half hour later he walked past his desk and his arm automatically dipped into the bowl and grabbed a piece of candy! It was very obvious that my friend was totally unaware of his "automatic" reaction. His mind said he was dieting and would not eat candy but his inner emotional self wanted to please his body. Sometimes we get disconnected from our emotional inner self. Often we decide what we want to do with our head but the reactions in our bodies can be different. When this happens we actually block ourselves from doing what the "head" decided to do.

It is not that difficult to get in touch with your inner self. Once you do that you can begin to understand your inner emotions and what truly motivates you. It is your inner self that really makes the big decisions in life. Once you integrate your Being (Higher Self) and your Body (your body personality in this life) you are able to know, understand and begin to assess how to take action to be successful. You can then be successful because then you are in alignment with all of your goals and you are not unconsciously blocking yourself.

One of the very first set of skills that enables you to see an aura is also the very skills needed to align yourself. These are the skills of grounding; running life force energy through your body and energy field to clear your space; centering your energy; and releasing old patterns and programs. These skills clear you and raise your vibration level so that your aura is cleaner, and your actions are in alignment with both your higher and lower natures.

SEEING THE INVISIBLE

It is not difficult to see an aura. It is easy. If you spend four or five months using a clairvoyant style meditation you will begin to see the colors that surround the human body. Anyone can do this. But you do have to be willing to spend the time to learn to focus your energy and to clear your space. Your space is your own aura that is your personal egg of light. To see someone else's aura you have to clear your aura so that you can see through it to see beyond yourself. Clearing your aura is releasing the memories of your past and heavy feelings of the present that stand in front of you and block your inner sight. As you clear the old patterns and images your energy vibration raises and your Higher Self can more easily communicate with you and sit in your body.

Your Higher Self can always see the aura. When you meet a new person your Higher Self will communicate with the other person's Higher Self. They will have an energy conversation. Usually they discuss past lives, where they knew one another in the past and what they can now learn or share with one another. If you meditate regularly and clear your energy you can be present enough to hear and know this conversation. This is part of what is meant when all of the major spiritual traditions encourage you to be in the PRESENT. The present is the ability to live in the now so that you are fully conscious of what both you the body and you the energy being are doing. It is the integration of spirit, mind and body. Once you have some of this integration you will begin to see the aura.

THE TRUTH FROM THE LIE

When a person lies his aura shakes. However, if there is more than forty percent truth in his lie then his aura will not shake. So if a person builds a lie around a truth it will seem true in his energy field!

Of course there are other energy skills for knowing when a person is not telling the truth. But these skills take a few years to develop, as the Reader has to be more integrated with his ability to see, hear and know his spiritual knowledge and to interpret this through his body.

THE POWER OF SEEING

Seeing the aura is only the very beginning of accessing inner awareness and moving towards the great goal of enlightenment. It is a tool and a wondrous life experience too. As you view the aura you come to understand the human condition, develop a deeper awareness of your own compassion and learn the age old skill of healing. Healing is the ability to move or shift energy to make a change.

CHAPTER THREE
YOUR BOOK OF LIFE

The amazing thing about the aura is that it holds the information of who you are and what your true potential is. When you are born there is a part of your aura we call the original aura or what your true potential is for this life. Some people accomplish their full potential in this life while others sometimes do not and so shuffle what they came to do to the next life. By looking at the original essential aura you came into this life with you can understand your true potential.

Your aura is your book of life. Although the chakras (the larger energy centers along your spine) are the true filing system for your life images), it is in your aura where the images that you are currently using are displayed. So when you decide to do something or take any kind of action the image of what you are placing into action moves from the chakra filing system out into your aura.

Reading the aura is more fun than reading a book or going to a movie or even accessing a historical record. By reading the aura you can actually read and see true history and how it affected a person.

THE QUICK SCAN

Often when people ask me to go to an event or party and read people's auras I have to do what is known as a quick scan. I have to look at a person's aura and determine what is happening for them in life determined by what their energy is doing at that particular moment. So I look to see if the person's aura reaches down to the ground and all the way around them. If the aura does not reach the ground then that person does not manifest many of their life desires. I look to see if the layers in the aura are of equal size or if some are larger while others are smaller. I scan to see what is very light and bright and beautiful and what is dark and hidden and feared or not working. First, of course, I like to look for what is this person's special skill or talent in life and if he is using it. Then I look for whether or not he is on his path in this life. Then, of course, I search out what the person's largest obstacle is at this time.

If you are an aura reader you quickly discover that most people want to know one simple thing about their health, their love life or their finances. Very few people ever ask a question about their spiritual life. Most people are concerned only with the practical aspects of their body personality in this life. But often, answering this simple question brings up many complex topics because in truth, everything is connected.

THE UPPER AND THE LOWER

The aura is an ovoid sphere, like an egg of energy that surrounds you. It is a few feet above you and extends a few feet below you into the earth. Very often when you look at an aura you will see a difference between the top and the bottom of the aura. The top half of the aura extends down to just above the heart. The bottom half of the aura extends from the heart down into the ground.

Many people who meditate learn a form of meditation that causes them to leave the body while meditating. This causes them to reach to higher levels of awareness but does not bring that higher consciousness into the body. So the top half of the aura gets clearer but the bottom half of the aura stays murky and un-cleared. The top half of the aura is considered the "spiritual" aura and is governed by the spiritual chakras, the Crown Chakra (on top of the head), the Sixth Chakra (the Third Eye in the forehead) and the Fifth Chakra (located in the throat.) If a person's meditation only governs their spiritual life then only these chakras and aura layers are cleared. This is the reason that many students of meditation have a wonderful experience while meditating and then come back into their bodies to discover they have many typical life problems—financially, health wise or problems with family or relationships. This is the very reason that at

Clearsight we developed a clairvoyant system of meditating that enables you to stay IN THE BODY while meditating and to channel your own life force energy throughout the entire body while doing that process. If you meditate while in the body you clear the entire body, both spiritual, emotional and physical. This allows the entire aura to clear and so causes your spiritual nature to align with your emotional and physical nature to integrate your many levels of consciousness.

Meditating is not just a process to feel good or to reach to a higher spiritual level of consciousness. Meditating should enable you to improve your life in every aspect. You are a spiritual being. You are just as spiritual when you are in your body as when you are out of it. This physical world we live in is part of the energy or spiritual realm and is also governed by those laws. Meditating is the act of clearing your energy and aligning yourself with the universal energy source. Meditating is a metaphysical science that allows humans to reach the divine and become one with it. If you do this while being IN your body you then empower yourself to create yourself as a consciously aware human being. You pull the thread of the divine consciousness throughout your entire body and your entire life process. This empowers you to act from your higher nature in a practical manner. This in turn allows you to discover your true compassion, your loving nature, and your ability to relate to others in a constructive manner, your free will and your ability to solve problems. And so this process evolves you to the next step of human consciousness and awareness. Once you learn to meditate in the body you also learn to stay in your body while you are awake. Most people do not have their astral and physical energy bodies aligned because they do not stay in their bodies while they are awake. Many people flit in and out of their bodies. Once you meditate enough in the body you learn to stay in your body all of your waking hours. This enables you to have a direct and immediate connection with your higher nature, your energy self, who is your divine director in life. Once truly connected on this level you make the right choices in life, have conscious awareness and are able to create the life you came here to experience.

WHAT DOES IT MEAN TO HAVE CONSCIOUS AWARENESS?

Conscious Awareness allows you to understand why specific situations happen in your life. There are no coincidences. Each person you meet you have usually met before in a previous life. It is rare to meet someone you have never seen or spoken to in a previous incarnation. Conscious Awareness allows you to know your past history with this person. This is valuable so that you understand the dynamics of your relationship. In this way you can finish karmic debts without repeating the same patterns. Conscious Awareness enables you to know when you are visiting a place that you have been to in a past life. It allows you to understand and know why something "seems similar."

Conscious Awareness is the first tool of the path of evolving your spiritual self to a higher clearer level. With the use of conscious awareness you can assess your health and know when your body is being stressed and take measures to release the stress before it severely impacts your body. Conscious Awareness connects you with your body as well as your Higher Self and your soul nature. So you just do not feel tired but know *why* you feel tired and what to do to regain your high energy. It allows you the ability to get information to enable you to shift out of old patterns, negative health situations and stuck relationships.

THE PAST, THE PRESENT AND THE FUTURE

Some energy workers believe that all experiences, all reality, happens at the same time. They believe that the universe operates on many levels simultaneously. I do not know if this is true or not. When I read the aura I see past lives, influences from a person's childhood and sometimes even future lives. These lives appear to be in a straight timeline but of course it is possible that on one level they are all happening at the same exact time and we simply perceive it as past, present and future. So far no one has been able to substantiate the theory of everything happening at one time. However it is a very fascinating concept that borders on advanced physics.

As Einstein put it when his great friend Michele Besso died: "People like us, who believe in physics, know that the distinction between past, present and future is only a stubbornly persistent illusion."

Lee Smolin, of the Perimeter Institute for Theoretical Physics in Canada, insists that "time is real" but says that reformulating it could be central to finding the long-sought "theory of everything" that unites all the forces and particles of the universe, notably by merging relativity and quantum theory.

When Clairvoyants read the aura they see past lives and notice how those past lives influence the present. When you need information about something you are experiencing in your life you will automatically unconsciously light up a past life in your aura. We call this "lighting up" because the image from that past life will appear as often looking like a bright stained glass window. Other times a past life will influence you because it carries some karma that is telling you to take some action in order to either right a wrong, or finish something carried over from the past, or to remember what you did before.

ANGER, FEAR, JEALOUSY---STRONG EMOTIONS

Most people are controlled by their emotions. Clairvoyant skills show you how to de-energize your emotions so that they do not control you. Everyone feels anger, fear, jealousy, love or many strong emotions at one time or another in their life. Your body is programmed to feel emotions. How you use your emotions and what you do with them is the issue in life.

Viewing the ovid sphere as a whole

The amazing thing about reading the aura is that you never know what you are going to see. It is an incredible experience of viewing colors, images and symbols that are almost beyond description. The colors are brilliant and brighter and clearer than physical colors. The images often show a story that extends from the far past to the present and even sometimes into the future. The symbols often teach the reader the keys to the very structure of life as we know it and so enhance your knowledge of the world beyond the physical. Reading the aura can be a positive life changing experience for both the Reader and the Readee.

As you view the aura as a whole there are certain very simple basics you can perceive. The energy above a person is what they are creating to bring into their life in the near future (two weeks to four months). Often people think they have released situations but simply move that energy down and out their aura into the ground. Sometimes that energy takes a long time to move out of the aura and often sits in the area around a person's feet (between the knee and the foot). What sits in the lower part of the aura is what is moving out or what can be temporarily stuck. Often when a person feels he is walking through mud he is actually walking through the sticky "mud" of his own past that has not yet released. When a reader sees this he can help the person to de-energize and release this energy.

How energy moves in the aura

The aura is always in motion. When you hear energy workers speak of a "block" in the aura they are simply speaking about some energy that is stuck and not moving. When this energy is stuck it is like a TV soap opera that gets stuck on the one same episode. When some issue in your aura does not move it cannot get cleared and you feed it and keep it happening. There are energy techniques for de-energizing stuck areas of the aura. Also, sometimes just by hearing about a stuck area brings it into the conscious level of awareness that allows a person to be aware enough to just shift it.

The relationship between the layers of the aura

There are seven basic layers in the aura. Within each layer there are also seven layers but Readers usually only read the seven basic layers. Readers trained in the Clearsight system read the layers because it is easier to get clear specific information in that manner. Many clairvoyants simply just read whatever they see. Sometimes they are intuitively led to the most important information but often they are reading randomly and haphazardly. Aura reading is a metaphysical science. By using your ability to look at specific areas of the aura you can quickly gather information and pinpoint certain recurring issues in a person's life.

Sometimes a person's layers will not be even. If a person is a performer, such as a singer or a comedian who is often in front of large audiences you will see that the seventh and the fifth layers are larger and more defined than the other layers. The Seventh outer layer protects the person while he is performing and the Fifth layer is the communication layer, which a performer uses more than the average person uses it. Similarly if the person is an athlete you will notice that the First Layer of the aura (physical layer) and the Third Layer (energy use) of the aura will be larger and stronger.

If you read for a few years to get experienced as a reader, you will notice that you can easily know certain things about a person from simply viewing the layers of the aura. For example, a martial artist has a very strong Third Layer of the aura. A Policeman also has a strong third layer but usually that layer is dark blue. Policemen have a defined morality, which translates into a deep blue color in the aura.

WHAT IS REALLY IMPORTANT TO THE PERSON YOU ARE READING

A clairvoyant reader of the aura is a person who can help the person being read by giving him information. A Reader does not try to influence a person but simply gives him information so that he can have more to work with to solve his life problems.

When you read an aura there is so much to look at. The aura is an incredible living book of a person's past, present and future. So the reader has to decide what to focus on in order to give the readee useful information.

Most people who want to get a reading do this to solve one particular problem in life. But the reader has a wider vantage point. The reader can give information that helps the person getting the reading to understand a situation and his own motivations. But the reader can also give the readee the information that enables him to see himself in the larger picture, the connection with his divine nature and his true purpose in this life. I have always trained readers to look for what kind of information will help the person they are reading to change their life for the better.

Many years ago a pretty young woman came to me in Tokyo for an aura reading. She put five pictures of men on the table and asked me which man she should marry. Her exact question was, "Which man is the best man to father a child with me?" I then asked her which man she loved. She told me that she did not love any of them but simply wanted to find a man to father a child with her. I then told her that none of these men were the right man and that she should find the man she loved. Of course you could hold the energy of each man and compare it with hers and find the best genetic match. But if there is no love the relationship would eventually fall apart and this would severely impact the child. A child born without love is a child who will eventually have a strained life.

It is true that many marriages do not work well these days. Even when a marriage starts with love and the best of intentions it can be difficult to keep that love and wonderment happening. But a marriage started with no love has not even a chance. So as a Reader I suggested that this woman find a man she loves to father a child with her. Of course she was very unhappy with my answer, as she simply wanted a quick designation of one of the photos as her potential child maker.

GIVING IS GETTING, READING IS LEARNING

Over the years we have discovered that as you read other people's auras you change and grow from that experience.

Our Clearsight system of reading the aura trains the reader to release any similar energy in his aura. As you read the aura you see your own similarities to the person you are reading and you use your energy skills to release them. So giving an Aura Reading can also be a way of clearing your own energy field and releasing your similar pictures. This means that each time you do an Aura Reading for someone you raise your own vibration level, get clearer, and so can see more easily. You grow spiritually, emotionally and so apply your skills to your own life while you are also helping another person understand their life. It is what we call in clairvoyant terminology, a win win situation. You learn and grow as you give out information that helps another person. This is why I really love using our particular Clearsight system of aura reading skills. These skills enable everyone to gain at the same time.

How a reading heals

By speaking aloud the information in a person's aura that the readee knows unconsciously but somehow cannot seem to rise to a conscious verbal level, the Reader allows the readee to heal himself. Simply by hearing this unsaid information it allows a person to further understand himself and to grow and change. Healing is another word for change. Healing is letting go of whatever blocks you to reach for a clearer perspective in life.

I had a woman come for a reading who had very bad feelings towards her mother. She felt that her mother was always critical of her and had been harsh towards her when she was a child. She told me that often she could still hear her mother's words still berating her for not being good enough. And sure enough, there were areas in her aura where she had held onto and stored her mother's words and energy. As she released this "foreign" energy from her aura she began to feel stronger and happier and stopped thinking about what her mother had said to her many years ago. Soon it was more important to her what she thought and felt about herself now than what her parent thought or stated to her in the past.

Change

Healing is the ability to move energy to cause a specific change within the body or the emotional or energy system of any living being. As you point out what images are within a person's aura it helps the person you are reading to understand and release old energies and to shift to new ways of behavior. When people hear their own aura read to them they start to understand their strengths and weaknesses. Often they feed their strength, own their abilities and release their fears and weaknesses.

You have choices in life. When someone Reads your aura they offer you the chance to understand yourself from a more powerful internal viewpoint and to choose what to let go of and what to keep and encourage in your life. Readings clarify life choices, allow people to see and know their full potential and to face and conquer their fears and denials. In the end people change quickly and easily and often have great personal revelations.

Several years ago I had a woman come to me for a Aura Reading in Tokyo. She immediately told me that she had been to me for a Reading over a year ago. "At that time", she said, "I could not understand a word you said. I left feeling I had wasted my time and money. Then I went home and a few months later I played the tape of our session. It took me another three months and then I began to understand what you were talking about. The things you told me totally changed my life for the better. I wanted to thank you for taking the time and effort to help me to see the true me, and my real potential. I feel that you must have realized I did not understand a word you said at the time but you were patient and made sure that you said all that I needed to hear. I really appreciate your care. Now I am back for the next step in my life. Only this time I feel I know how to hear what you are saying."

I was thrilled to hear this from my readee. Some people immediately hear and understand what is being told to them. But others often look blank and lost. I try to make sure that each person gets the deepest information I can give them that they can hear at the time of their reading. But sometimes you never get any feedback and just hope you have done well for that person. My karmic purpose in this life is to give information to people that will help them to grow spiritually and on every other level in their lives too. So hearing her story made me feel happy that I was reaching people well.

LIFE FORCE ENERGY

Your aura is your life force energy. It is you in action. What you do with your energy is how you create your life. As you begin to see your own and other's auras you learn how your energy works, how it behaves, how it moves and how you can use it to make your dreams come true in this life and in the next one too.

CHAPTER FOUR
FREE WILL, DESTINY &
YOUR CHOICES IN LIFE

DESTINY

Many people are born and spend their entire lives asking questions about who they are and why these things happen to them. Once you open yourself to the world of spirituality you come to understand that nothing is without a cause or reason. Every person you meet and encounter is a learning experience for you. Every situation happens for a reason, which is usually to teach you something or to clean up old karma.

Old karma are debts you have or unfulfilled agreements or actions. In the spiritual language of Sanskrit, which the word karma comes from, the basic definition of karma is to take action. The results of your action cause an affect, which is what most modern New Age people define karma as. At Clearsight we tend to use three simple definitions: cause and affect, unfulfilled agreements or debts and the actions you do to cause the life you have. So karma can be what you do but it can also be just what you think. All that you do and think is a karmic action that causes your life to be the way it is now. You are the creator of your karma and the person who can fulfill or clear it.

FREE WILL

I have a client who was happily married. Her husband earned a good salary and she did not have to go out to work. But my friend wanted a challenge in life. She wanted to feel that she was accomplishing something. So she decided to open a small business. She asked her husband what he thought of her working and he told her that he would support her in doing whatever made her happy. So my client opened a small business. She started a magazine for parent and children activities. Theoretically it should have been a very successful business. There was a market for it and my client researched it thoroughly and did all of the right things. But she failed. She felt poorly about failing but was determined to find the right successful business to open. So she found a business consultant to give her seasoned advice. Then she opened a business in catering. She had always been a good cook and loved to hold parties for her friends. She felt that this business was just the right one for her. But after eight months of struggle she failed once again. Having a strong nature to make something work she tried one more business, a referral business for part time workers. And she failed at this too.

My client then went to her business consultant and asked him what she had done wrong. She did not want to consider herself a failure at business. Her business consultant told her that she had done nothing wrong. She had started and performed all of the businesses properly. He finally told her that it was not the business but her that had something wrong. And not being able to know or see what was wrong he finally suggested that she consult a Clairvoyant Reader to see into her reason for failing. And that was when she became my client.

My client had done nothing wrong in business. Matter of fact, she had done everything right to be a very successful business manager. She had done everything right except for one thing. And that one thing turned out to be the most important thing that anyone can know and do. My client had not connected with herself well enough to know herself and so she was not on her path. She was not being true to her real purpose for being here in this life. She was just simply trying to make money doing a business. But truly, this is not what life is really all about!

Almost anyone who has studied any spiritual, metaphysical or religious practices has heard the phrase, "Know thyself." But often people do not really understand what this actually means. It is not just knowing your favorite food, most liked environment, favorite vacation spot and likes and dislikes about people or relationships. It is not just knowing what we call your body personality---who you are in this life. It is knowing your spiritual purpose for reincarnating in this body. What did you come here to learn and accomplish in this life? Every single thing that is a part of you---a part of your creation is put in place for a purpose. If you are thin or fat, if you have a fast or slow metabolism, if you have a striking beauty about you or a cuteness or a deformity or handicap, it is there to teach you something. You learn through your physical body in this life but you learn a spiritual lesson. Your spiritual lesson enhances and enlightens you as an energy Being.

My client's path in this life was to aid and help people. Somehow she did not see doing a magazine for parents and children or a catering business as "helping" people. Of course these businesses do create a service that helps people but in some manner this did not fit her inner concept, her spiritual path in this life and so she failed at it. Slowly my client started to meditate and learn to look within herself. She learned how to align herself with her higher nature, her Higher Self, and then the answer came to her. She created a business that did make money but its basic purpose was *not* to make money. It's basic purpose was to create a better world by sending experts into third world countries with new and cheap technology for creating clean wells. And now her business is successful and her spirit is happy.

Very often in the modern world we create a lifestyle that is based upon earning money and creating goods. We sometimes get out of touch with what really makes us happy and fulfilled. We often get caught up in simply earning a living and staying financially afloat. And then we come to think of this as our purpose. But it is your higher purpose, your spiritual purpose, that gives you the true drive to accomplish both your survival and greater things in life.

You do not live to work. You do not live just to survive. You are here to learn and grow and give aid and help by your clear example to everyone around you. We all learn from one another. When you clear your aura, get in touch with your soul consciousness and get to a higher level of awareness everyone around you will try to match you. One clear person in a room creates everyone else in the room trying to reach that same clear potential. Just by clearing your aura and connecting with your soul consciousness you are raising the energy on the planet.

As your aura clears you become more of a being of light. You become a channel of the light and you spread this consciousness wherever you go. So each one of us is the potential of evolution on the human race and the spirit of all energy.

So many young people choose their careers or work lives by what their parent's do or what their parents want them to do. Some choose their work life by what pays the most or what is the most popular career path when they graduate from school. What you work at is what you do for the greater majority of time during your day. Most people work somewhere from forty to sixty hours per week. If you are not happy at your work, not satisfied or fulfilled by it and not aligned with your true nature spiritually you will be uncomfortable. This discomfort sits under the surface in the emotional second layer of your aura and the action third layer of your aura and you feel at odds with yourself. It affects you in everything you do. When you are constantly uncomfortable you interpret it as a failure in your life and you do not trust your feelings and trash yourself internally.

Not everyone has the privilege or timing to work at the perfect job. If you have worked for years at a specific job that you really do not connect with sometimes you cannot quit or change late in life. If that happens then you look to find some other hobby, interest, or action that allows you to connect with your true purpose in life. I have had several clients who woke up one day to realize that their jobs were truly unfulfilling but financially good for their families.

We often speak of purpose, mission, path or the quest to find the revelation in your life that connects you with your inner and Higher Self that allows you to be in the balanced conscious state of awareness. In the past we often believed that only the priests in the temples, the monks, nuns and spiritual people who devoted every moment of their lives to a spiritual state of consciousness could reach a level of enlightenment or what we clairvoyants called "conscious awareness."

We have since learned that there are many levels of enlightenment and that you can connect with this and experience it in daily life. You do not have to sit in the temple or shrine on the mountain or cloister yourself in the monastery to achieve the spiritual state of awareness. Matter of fact, most of us are here to achieve this in daily life so we help to evolve the human race and shift to a higher level. We are here to evolve but also to share that evolution with one another as we learn and grow.

Ownership of energy

Your aura is your personal universe. Whatever is in your aura is what you will create in your life. Some people have not learned how to own their aura and so they pick up other people's energy as if they are a universal sponge. This often happens to people who are too empathetic and want to help others but do not know how or what to do.

Your aura is you own personal sphere of life force energy. This is the energy that came into your body when you were born. Only your own energy should be in your aura. Whatever is in your aura is what you create in your life. You created this body to learn and experience and so you should be the person who decides what you do and how you do it. Therefore only your own energy should be within your own aura.

Reaching your higher self

There are many skills and techniques that create the ability for the average person to evolve and integrate with their Higher Self. Reading the aura is one of these techniques. Over the years many people have come into our Clairvoyant School to read the aura so they can see their friend's auras, use it in business, be more successful and release restricting patterns and fears. And learning to read the aura does enable you to do all of these things. But the real reason I started to teach reading the aura is that it is one of the quickest ways to enable a person to evolve and integrate with their Higher Self. Many spiritual paths take years of practice to get to the same level.

Reading the aura means you have to clear your own aura to see through it in order to see the other guy's aura. This means that every time your read the aura using the Clearsight method of de-energizing your own images you get clearer and raise yourself to a higher level. The process of Reading the Aura that we have developed enables you to clear yourself while giving another person the information they seek. So while giving information you too get information. It is what we call a win win situation. Just by reading using this process you evolve yourself into a higher consciousness.

There is you, the Higher Self, which is the part of you that created this body to learn and grow in. And then there is you, the Body Personality, the part of you that is born into a particular body in this life and the personality that has developed through your body. When you meditate and integrate your Higher Self and your Body Personality you come into a oneness. While in this state of oneness you can easily read an aura, know and understand your self, be intuitive and consciously aware and connect with the universal life source. Integrating body and spirit brings about the first stages of enlightenment. It is your Higher Self that can show you your true path in life. It is your body personality that can put it into action. It is the integration that can bring about the calmness, and the joining with the cosmic oneness that leads you to your evolution.

YOUR CHOICES IN LIFE

By understanding your motivations and what causes you to act the way you do, you can also choose whether to follow these "feelings" and "emotions" or to use your clairvoyant skills to release them and choose another path. By understanding your inner self, the true keys to your motivations, you also have the choice to change your actions. You can de-energize your fears, your emotions and your traumatic memories that drive you to action. You can release the trauma that feeds your actions. You can choose what kind of person you want to be and what kind of actions you want to take. You then are in charge.

PRACTICAL USES OF CLAIRVOYANT ENERGY WORK

When I first started teaching people how to read the aura in 1979 I was young and excited about showing people how to see colors and images. I had no idea of the power of seeing an aura. I just thought it was fun, easy to do and opened a fascinating door to the world of energy. It took me the first two years of teaching clairvoyancy to realize the true relevance of these marvelous life skills.

I watched my students change. As they learned our Clearsight skills they became more successful at their jobs. They developed new relationship skills and came to understand the people in their lives on a much deeper level. As they changed and grew they started to understand and know themselves in a way that increased their natural power. Literally their auras became balanced and stronger and they became charismatic people. I saw shy people become powerful managers in offices. I discovered that the very assertive and sometimes arrogant people became humble, caring and compassionate as they became truly aware of what other people felt inside. I watched people who had little self-esteem grow into strong healthy well rounded outgoing people who learned to love both themselves and others.

For me it was an incredible learning experience to see what using clairvoyant skills could give to people. In all ways these skills improved people's lives and gave them the extra sense of consciousness that is so valuable in every way in our modern and changeable world. And so I would like to share with you a few stories of how we clairvoyants use our skills in daily life.

MOVING THE FIRE

I live in the Santa Monica mountains, a nature canyon filled area about one hour's drive north of Los Angeles. I have always chosen to live as close to nature as possible and yet have access to a city where I can teach and also shop. Eight years ago I lived in an area called Agoura and this whole area near the coast has what we call two seasons, fire and flood. My home, being up on a hillside had no problems with floods but fire was a constant threat.

About eight years ago I was driving on my way to visit my father in the San Fernando Valley. As I passed an area called Calabasas I noticed smoke and what seemed like a small fire. It used to take about forty minutes to drive to see my father and as I drove I was listening to the local news station. Suddenly an announcement came on about the Calabasas fire and how it was fast growing in strength and moving northwards. The winds were very strong that day as often they can be in Southern California. I immediately pulled over and called my neighbors. We lived further north of Calabasas but fire can easily travel very fast overland through the brush areas. My neighbors told me that the smoke was very visible and that the fire was being fanned by strong winds, and moving very fast, coming right towards our area. Although the fire was still more than three canyons away, they suggested that I drive home immediately. From past experience I knew that once fire moved into an area it was difficult to get back to your home. The fire department would set up fire lines and refuse to let you into the area. So I turned around and drove home.

By the time I got home the fire was consuming homes south of us and crossing the wild lands very fast. Smoke and dry ash was already in the air. My home was the only home in the entire area with a roof sprinkler so I turned that on. But the winds were so hot and dry that as soon as the water hit the roof and the front stairs it was evaporating.

I turned on the TV. I lived in a small cottage and you could watch the TV and at the same time, if you kept the front door open you could also see the fire which was now about two canyons away and moving fast. I had a houseguest staying with me who was a graduate of our program. He and I watched the TV and listened to the announcements of where the fire was moving. The local high schools had set up evacuation centers for residents who lived in the path of the fire. Usually the firemen requested that people leave their homes so that the firemen could fight the fire without worrying about saving people.

Three canyons were involved and in the path of the fire. People were moving horses and animals from the canyons to safe spots set up to take care of animals. One of my students living in Topanga, a canyon closer to the fire, called me. She had decided to stay in her home. I strongly encouraged her to go to the evacuation station at the High School in Agoura. She refused. She told me that the fire engines were now right outside of her home. This worried me because that meant that her home was directly in the current path of the fire. The fire engines only go right to the spot where they can be set up to best fight the fire. So I felt she was in immediate danger. But she refused to leave and there was nothing I could do. I have never liked feeling powerless. And so I started to think if there was anything that could be done in this situation.

It was at that point that my house guest and I decided that there was something we could do. We could use our energy skills to fight the fire. As we listened to the announcer he told us exactly where the fire was located and what was happening with it. And so the two of us sat down, did out process of Running Energy and started to look clairvoyantly at the fire energy. We could not "fight" the fire. But we could use the ancient elemental Eco-Spirit techniques to move it. And so we focused on the ancient skill of becoming the fire and then moving it in another direction. It was an amazing experience for both of us. As we moved the fire back towards the south the announcer came on the TV saying, "Now the fire is moving back on itself. We do not know why but it has changed direction going back to where it was before." We kept this up for about twenty minutes and then we got a little tired and a bit complacent and we stopped. We could not stop the fire but we had realized that we could move it and shift it and so buy some time as it reburned the same area it had been in before. About ten minutes after we stopped working on the fire and were relaxing the announcer stated that the fire had once again started moving northwards at a fast pace being fanned by the now very strong Santa Ana Winds.

Once again we sat down, and proceeded to become the fire energetically and so move the fire in a southerly direction again. We did this throughout the afternoon and each time we stopped the fire would come back towards the north. It was obvious that our ploy was working. But eventually the winds grew much worse and even our energy work would not help. Luckily at sundown the winds died down and shifted. The fire was finally contained about two canyons from us. We were spared. Our student in Topanga was OK too.

But the big hero of the day was our teacher, Mark. Mark lived much further away from us, further south about 40 miles down the coast in Laguna Beach. Due to the Santa Ana fierce winds Laguna Beach also had a fire at the same time as ours. Mark lived up in the canyons overlooking the beach in a small building with about eight apartments. When the fire started moving towards Mark's home he left his apartment, ran up to the roof with a hose and held off the fire preventing it from burning the apartment house he lived in. We considered this incredibly courageous and a bit foolish too. Fire moves down a hillside in about eight minutes. It is not the fire that is so dangerous to people. It is the heated air and the smoke that can enter your lungs and kill you very quickly. Mark risked his life to save his apartment building. The owner of the building adored him and was forever thankful. We know that Mark used his clairvoyant skills when he fought the fire. Mark is our Male Energy Teacher, a professional healer and a very astute businessman. Mark has told me many stories of how he uses his clairvoyant skills all of the time, in business meetings, on social occasions and for healing and teaching too. So I am sure his ability to stay grounded, to de-energize his fear and panic and to stay focused helped him to fight the fire. Having clairvoyant skills really does give you an edge in disaster situations. If you can stay grounded and keep your head clear and not fall into panic and fear you can often do better in any disaster or scary situation that comes your way!

FINDING A LOST CAT

One day a member of our Clearsight Staff came to see me. She was very upset. Her cat was missing. It had gotten out of her apartment and was nowhere to be found. Over the years I have had many kitties as pets so I am very familiar with finding lost cats. She had searched everywhere within an eight block radius in all directions. She had asked her neighbors and anyone who might have been in the area or seen the cat. But no one had seen the cat and she did not know what to do. She had checked the animal shelters but no cat of her description had been turned in. She was very afraid her cat had been hit by a car and was very hurt or not alive anymore.

I told her how to do a CALL BACK for her kitty and got the name and description of her cat so I could also do this for her too. There are two basic ways I find a lost animal. I use clairvoyant techniques to see the animal. Having its name and description helps me to know I am looking at the right cat. Then I put an energy bowl of milk or food in front of it and move the bowl towards it's home. I use this to entice it to come home. When you feed an animal it sets up a belief that you love them and care about them. And so it always sets up a pattern of return. If you feed a stray cat it will return to you again. Food reminds the cat that it is missed and will be cared for if it gets home. This works as long as the animal knows its way home.

Sometimes animals get so lost that even with their marvelous sense of smell and direction they cannot find their way home. If I think that this is the case then I look at the cat and expand my awareness to see where the cat is. Since the animal is low I start to look upwards to find a street sign, business sign or some specific landmark so the owner can go to this site, call the cat and retrieve it. Since cats in particular are afraid of noise, cars and strange people, they tend to hide. So when you go to the area you have to be a person it knows and you have to gently call it to you.

Two days after we did a CALL BACK she found the cat right outside of her building. She was lucky that the cat knew its way home. Our Staff person was very happy. She had feared her cat was dead. But the very first thing I did when she had contacted me was to look clairvoyantly to see if the cat was alive. Once I could see it was alive I knew that we had a good chance of bringing it back home with a CALL BACK. A CALL BACK is not a direct clairvoyant skill. It is a very ancient pagan skill that is much easier to use if you are clairvoyant and can see the energy of the animal you are trying to recover.

THE STOLEN MOTORCYCLE

About eight years ago I had a student in Tokyo whose older brother often made fun of her for studying clairvoyancy. My student was a very capable graduate in one of our advanced programs. Her brother refused to listen to whatever she would say about studying clairvoyancy. He believed it was not real and therefore was a waste of time. She had tried many times to explain to him about the value of clairvoyant insight but his mind was closed to whatever she would say. Then one day her brother had his motorcycle stolen. He was very distraught. His sister, wanting to help him, so she looked clairvoyantly to see where the motorcycle was. She found the area and the street name and told her brother to go there and that he would find his stolen motorcycle. He thought she was totally crazy but to humor her he went to the place she suggested. And lo and behold, there was his motorcycle, which he immediately took home with him. And then her brother wanted to know how she had found his motorcycle! She told him that she had used her clairvoyant skills to find the motorcycle and that she was happy that it worked for him. He was flabbergasted. Her brother had a great deal of trouble simply excepting her explanation. To him, it was as if she had pulled this information out of thin air! But my graduate student was very capable. She had learned the skill of focusing her energy to look for something and had used her clairvoyant skills to search and find. From then on her brother held her in great respect and stopped making fun of his younger sister for being involved in "this waste of time weird stuff."

THE MISSING DRESS

One of our graduate students is a dress designer. One day she was transporting some dresses to a fashion show and somehow in the frenetic movement one dress got left in the taxicab. This dress was a special and very expensive designer dress. Someone else had paid for the cab so she did not have a receipt to trace to the cab company. She came to me in a panic. She was very distraught and was sure she would lose her job and have to pay for the very expensive dress too. She was in tears and did not know what to do. I simply suggested she use her clairvoyant skills to calm herself and get into a clear state of awareness. Then I suggested she do what we use for animals when they are lost, which is what we call, A CALL BACK. To do this you have to be calm, release all of your hysterical or emotional energy and then pull the energy of the animal or object back to you. If an object belongs to you then it will return to you if this CALL BACK is done properly. At first she was too distraught to consider this but soon she realized that really she had no other options. Since this was the only path of opportunity left to her she focused herself and used her skills.

Three days later she came back to our Center and was all smiles. The cab company had returned the dress. Somehow they had traced it back to her office address. It was returned in such a way that her boss never even realized it was missing. She was ecstatic. She could not figure out how the cab company had managed to find her. "It was magic," she told me. "No, it was your use of skills and ownership of your power," I told her. Clairvoyant skills are truly marvelous when they work!

FINDING A PERSON

We have a person on the Board of Directors of our Clearsight School who is really good at being able to concentrate and use his clairvoyant skills. He is what people call a natural clairvoyant since he does this naturally and easily without any effort. One day a friend came to him to say that someone in her group was missing. She asked him if there was any chance he could find this young man.

Our Clairvoyant asked her to bring him a piece of clothing belonging to the missing young man. He took the clothing, held it in his hand, and grounded himself and used our Clearsight technique of Running Energy and De-Energizing Mental Image Pictures to clear his space of any extraneous thoughts that might cloud his perceptions. Then he concentrated in a very deep fashion.

After a few minutes our clairvoyant asked for a map of the United States. We were in California at the time. He spread out the map, and pointed to a different State called Arizona. He then asked for a detailed Arizona map. With total certainty he pointed to a particular street, put his hand on the corner of the intersection and explained that the person being sought was in a house on that corner. Sure enough it turned out to be entirely correct. The next day the people searching verified they had found the person they were looking for exactly where he had sent them.

Clairvoyant skills can be amazing

Over the years I have seen people use clairvoyant skills that are remarkable and completely unbelievable but true. I have seen clairvoyants correctly predict earthquakes down to the date, time, place and magnitude. Though these people usually do this once, they often cannot do it consistently unfortunately. I have seen people take a letter sent to someone at a far distance and read it exactly word for word without ever seeing the contents of the letter. I have known clairvoyants who found artifacts in Egypt at ancient sites by simply knowing where they are located from a past life they had in Egypt. This even startled the Egyptians who had seen many archaeologists scan the site but could not find the artifacts that the clairvoyants find without maps, digging or archaeological schooling. Truly not everyone can do this. Some people have acquired and carried on these skills from a past life. Others simply tune in to their true potential and discover that they can do incredible things as they learn to empower themselves. We are energy beings and once we own that concept and allow ourselves to know and use our energies we can transcend space and time to get wondrous information in a usable fashion.

KNOWING IF SOMEONE IS ALIVE OR DEAD

One day I was visiting at the home of a friend of mine in Northern California who is a very famous professional clairvoyant psychic. We were having tea when there was a knock on the door. A young man came in. He seemed very emotionally distraught. He explained to us that he was friends with a family that had a missing daughter. She had disappeared a week ago and no one had heard from her since. She was the kind of daughter who kept in constant contact with family and friends. Her family was sure she had met with foul play. He pleaded with us to try to find any information the family could use to find their daughter.

And so the first thing we did was to clear ourselves of all extraneous thought and look to see if she was still alive. Almost instantaneously I found her in the overworld. It was obvious that she no longer had a live body. These kinds of cases are so sad. Obviously she had been murdered. I do not like to look at dead bodies so I am not good at finding a body. My friend could not see where she was either. A week later we heard that a local psychic school had used over twelve Readers to piece together enough information to find the general area where her body was buried. They told this to the police who then did indeed find her body buried in a state park as the psychics had described!

There is a distinctive energy pattern when a person is in the overworld and does not have a live body anymore! Many people space out during the daytime hours and leave their bodies and go astral traveling. People especially do this in classrooms, in auditoriums, in large business gatherings when they are bored. But their energy looks different when they no longer have a body to return to. Clairvoyant training teaches you to stay in your body while you are awake. This makes you more capable and gives you the ability to have conscious awareness. Conscious Awareness allows you to get information while awake in a conscious state. This is the kind of information that clairvoyants and psychics receive that enables them to "pull the answers out of thin air!" Clairvoyant skills are a metaphysical science that anyone can learn to do and use.

CHANGING THE ENERGY IN A SITUATION

Several years ago a former student came to visit me. She was totally stressed out and told me she was at the end of her ability to deal with a situation at work. She loved her work and got along well with most of her working companions except for one. It seemed there was this one man who was a supervisor that she felt was purposefully abusing her in a sexist manner.

Her words went like this, "He makes sly insinuations and whispers strange things to me when no one else can hear. I feel he is coming on to me in a very sleazy way. He does this in a way that no one else hears or notices what he says. Every day I find it harder and harder to go to work and wonder if I should just quit. I have a good job and have spent years with this company. I have worked my way up to a very good position. I do not know what I will do if I have to quit. "

I asked her if she wanted to file a complaint about her "sexist" supervisor. She told me that he was very careful to whisper things only to her and that she had no actual proof to show what he was doing. She also emphatically told me that she did not want to get involved in a lawsuit. She felt it would embarrass the company and that even if she won she would lose her job anyway.

Her question to me was, "What should I do? What can I do?"

I told her to do two things that I thought would work in the situation.

This is exactly what I told her. "First of all you have to get into what we call neutral. I can see you have very strong feelings about this man. When you speak your face shows me that you are angry and hurt and really feel abused by his actions.

I am going to tell you a way to move him out of your life. What you want is for him to not be in your universe. This is a simple and easy way to do this. But you must be in neutral when you do this.

Sit down and give this man a long distance healing. Do a full healing to the very best of your ability. You want to shift his energy to raise it to a higher vibration level so that he shifts into his next level of learning. Do not put in any of your beliefs or feelings into this. Heal him in a totally neutral fashion. Give him the same level of deep healing you would give to your best friend. To do this you must stay in neutral. You must clear all of your feelings about this man and simply heal him to make him a clearer better person. You must heal him in a totally positive manner to help him shift his energy to a higher level.

Now you also have to take care of yourself. After you do the healing get yourself a massage, take a good hot bath with some wonderful aromatherapy goods, and do whatever you need to do to truly relax yourself. Have faith. Clear yourself as best as possible to release your panic and stress. Do some exercise and get in touch with your body and just do whatever you can do regain your inner sense of strength."

Two weeks later my student called me. She was ecstatic. It seemed that some higher up executive had noticed this gentleman's sales ability and had decided to move him to another section of the company. He got a promotion. My student no longer had to see or interact with him. He no longer ever visited or supervised her section of the company. He had simply moved out of her universe.

I told her that this was the positive way to deal with such a situation. I also told her that I thought that if he continued to harass women in this manner eventually he would either leave himself open to being prosecuted or somehow the karma would catch up with him. But I also told her that I was really proud of her actions. She had dealt with the situation in a positive way and had used her skills to create the kind of world she wanted to have without damaging the company or using dark or negative energy to deal with it. She had simply moved this man out of her personal world. And she did this by shifting his energy to a higher vibrational level. We can only hope that at a higher level he would also shift his sexist negative behavior too, or perhaps just be too busy at his new job to harass others. But regardless, if you can use positive energy to deal with a negative situation you are always in a good place. She used her skills in the very best way possible and so got a great result.

FINDING YOUR MATE

About seven or eight years ago I had this interesting experience. One night, after a clairvoyant practice in Tokyo, three of my male graduate students independently came to see me one by one. Each one of them was asking me the same question. How can I find a mate? None of them were aware of the others but somehow coincidentally they were all at that point in their life when they wanted to find a woman to relate to. Each young man told me that he had difficulty finding the right woman.

Often students ask me how to solve a problem as if they have no skills and no knowledge of how to solve their problem. I was amazed and simply looked at each one, as I was perplexed. And so I told them to "simply use your skill. De-energize your past experiences and your stories of how difficult this is. You know the skill of how to do what we call "a mock up," which you learned in the very first seminar of the Clairvoyant Program. This is a skill of how to create getting whatever you need in life. "Use that skill. But be clear about exactly what you want. Know yourself, and know what type of woman you want to relate to and then it will work."

All three men went home to do mock-ups. Five weeks later each man came to me and told me that he had found the love of his life. They thanked me for reminding them to use their skills. One of these men now has a professional alternative healing practice and two beautiful children who visit me every few years. The other two are happily married.

CREATING ABUNDANCE IN YOUR LIFE

When you clear old energy out of your aura new experiences can move in. If you have the courage to change you can bring more into your life. When I first started teaching Clairvoyancy in 1979 people would tell me that they did not want to study meditation because it was "boring." However, meditation is a main key to changing your life, your health and well-being and your ability to create abundance in your life. As you find a clear space in your inner world you are removing all of the blocks, the flotsam and jetsam that coats you with useless debris that prevents you from making a direct connection with the world and shifting your position in life. Meditation creates a calmness that clears you and allows you to assess yourself from a deeper viewpoint and so gives you the space to create your true priorities in life.

At Clearsight we practice a clairvoyant meditation that uses gold energy to clear the body. Over the years we have noticed that people who practice this energy meditation using gold cosmic energy increase their success ratio dramatically. We attribute this to clearing your space, to getting in touch with the true you and also to using gold energy. In the metaphysical world gold is considered the highest vibration energy you can use in a body.

Energetic skills, such as seeing and healing the aura, can dramatically improve your life if you use them consistently throughout your day as a normal part of your lifestyle.

Solving health issues

Last year one of my students came to me during an evening practice. She told me that she had been having a pain in her lower abdomen and so had gone to a doctor. The doctor had discovered a tumor in her ovary. The doctor had done a blood test and did not think it was cancerous but did think it could continue to grow and give her pain and be a problem if it continued to get much larger. She told me she was scared and worried and ask me if there was anything she could do using energy to heal this health problem.

I told her to de-energize her fears and worries and then to use our healing skills to work on the tumor to get rid of it. I suggested she drain the energy out of the tumor and to fill in the area with cosmic love energy. Love heals. Then I told her to shrink the tumor. I suggested that she do this three or four times a day or whenever she had a moment.

One month later my student called the doctor to have another exam of her problem. The doctor told her that usually they wait three months before re-examining the size of a tumor. My student insisted on having an appointment and being re-examined. Upon examination the tumor had virtually disappeared. The doctor was shocked because this rarely happened in such a short period of time. My student, however, understood that she had taken power over her body and her life. She had used her energy to create a healthy body. By focusing on shrinking her tumor she had empowered herself with the ability to own her body. Now she felt healthy and strong and believed in herself and her ability to create a healthy world for herself and her family. She had learned a most powerful skill, the skill of personal empowerment using your own energy

Chapter Five
Healing With Inner Sight

Healing using your inner sight

Several years ago a woman took our Clearsight Clairvoyant Program who had a panic disorder. She was frightened when she left her home and especially frightened when she would ride trains or a subway. But she managed to get to our classes and learned the basic skills for seeing the aura. As she learned to see other people's aura she also learned to see her own aura. She found that her aura had many fear pictures of her stepfather. Her mother had remarried when she was a young child and she did not get along well with her stepfather. As she de-energized the fear images in her aura her panic decreased. Soon she was able to travel in the subways, ride the trains and leave her home without experiencing the all invading panic she was so used to feeling. Other students in the class noticed the change in her as her facial features relaxed and her face began to mirror the beauty that was within her. She moved in a more relaxed manner and projected a warm essence instead of the strained panic look she used to exude. By learning to see her aura she learned to find the energy that blocked her and simply released it. This changed her entire outlook in life. It allowed her to live without the fears that had controlled her.

Your aura is the energy that protects you but it is also the energy that holds your feelings, your unconscious thoughts and your fears. Sometimes we are aware of our fears and our "stuck places" and sometimes we are oblivious to them. By seeing the aura we are forced to acknowledge this energy but can also quickly and instantaneously release it. No one wants to look at their fears so we bury them where we will not see them. But our fears still affect and control us. When you view the aura you can see these fears as energy and you can release that energy *before* you start to feel it.

HEALERS AND THE AURA

Clairvoyant Healers clean the aura in order to heal people. They remove all foreign energy and anything a person is ready to let go of. They also smooth and balance the aura. A healthy aura moves like a flowing river. When something gets stuck the aura moves more slowly or stops moving in some areas. A healer removes or shifts the stuck energy so that the aura is balanced and moving. Anyone can learn to see an aura or to feel an aura and be an Aura

Healer. Healing the aura is a skill that anyone who takes the time to practice and study can learn.

Foreign energy is a message that does not fit so it is discordant and unbalances your system. Many people do not understand the concept of ownership and so easily pick up someone else's energy. When you are born your life force energy enters your body. This is the energy that holds your particular life patterns. It is the energy version of DNA. This energy floods down through the baby's body flowing through the two energy channels along the spine and going through the seven basic energy centers (chakras). As the energy flows through these chakras it spins out around the body and forms the seven layers of the aura. This life force energy is coded and particular to the new baby, the new person to be. This is the energy that is always in affinity with your body. If someone else's energy should get stuck in this energy field it has what we call a different vibration and different programs so it does not keep with the original plan of the physical body. Foreign energy in the aura gives off different messages that blocks the true purpose of what you came here to do. Clairvoyant healers have discovered that probably eighty percent of illness is simply caused by foreign energy in a person's energy field (aura).

Sometimes a person's own energy will block the movement of his aura. The aura is always in constant movement. When the aura stops moving or becomes blocked in some area that sends a message to the body and discordance, unbalance or illness starts to occur.

WORKING WITH ENERGY IS EASY

I have always been amazed at how simple and easy it is to work with energy. I used to love to play racquetball. But though I really enjoyed playing I was never very good at it. Somehow I would often miss hitting the ball back. It was as if my arm would just not hit straight on. One day while playing I noticed that there seemed to be some energy stuck at my elbow. I looked at it clairvoyantly and noticed that there was some energy from my grandmother that had somehow gotten stuck in my elbow. I only remember meeting my grandmother once. She passed away when I was quite a young child. But somehow some of her energy had gotten left and stuck in my elbow chakra. I immediately pulled out my grandmother's energy from my elbow and sent it back to her. (This energy would return to her Higher Self wherever she is, as this is her life force energy.) From that day on I hit the balls well and became a much better racquetball player. My arm seemed straightened and felt quite different as if it were stronger and more easily directed. To me the difference was amazing. But the really amazing thing about this is that all I did was recognize that there was foreign energy in my elbow and removed it in less than a minute. I have always loved working with energy because it is so easy and quick to make significant changes. When you work with energy it is effortless. If you direct energy to move then it moves. For me, working with energy has always been a powerful and fun way to change my life and improve my health.

EMOTIONS THAT YOU FEED

Whenever you keep thinking about something you are feeding it. People tend to feed whatever they are afraid of or their deep emotional memories. By feeding your fear with energy you are making it stronger so that it becomes a larger part of your reality. This is why there are many therapists and coaches who will tell you to "think positively." You want to think of what you want to create. This makes your energy become stronger. When your energy is creating it is occupied getting something done! Being creative also boosts your energy to a higher energy level. When you think of what you do not have your aura turns darker. When people concentrate on what they do not have their aura turns a dark blue. Dark blue is also the color of depression and sadness. When you aura turns a dark color you are at a lower vibration and have less ability to create what you want! When you spend a great deal of time thinking about your fears your aura turns grayish-red. When you act out of fear you energy is restrictive and sometimes even paralyzed which then stops you from taking action to get what you want. Psychiatrists, psychologists and therapists, as well as coaches and Clairvoyants will tell you to teach yourself to create and feed positive thinking. When you think positively and take action to do something or solve a problem your aura gets light and bright.

PICTURES THAT GET STUCK IN THE AURA

There are images within your aura that are the story of your identity—who you are. These images that Clairvoyants call pictures also motivate you to act in certain ways.

If you have a "shy picture," and it is energized or what Clairvoyants call "lit up" you will act shyly. If you have a picture of a fear in your aura and it gets triggered you will go into fear. Pictures become energized for several different reasons. You can have a picture get filled with energy when you are searching for an answer of how to deal with a particular situation. Your energy self will light up (fill with energy so it is bright and charged) a past life picture of how you dealt with this situation; or an image of how you dealt with this in your recent past in this life. This is done unconsciously. Once this image is charged your aura will continue to fill it full of energy as your aura moves and you will unconsciously act off of it. The action you take in a situation will be whatever is in the image. Images also get charged in your aura when they are triggered in specific situations. For example: if you are afraid of spiders but never encounter a spider the picture will remain dormant and probably stored in your chakra. But if you should be cleaning your home and suddenly discover a spider it will trigger the fear picture. The image will then move from your chakra into your aura and feed you the message of fear.

Sometimes these images get stuck in your aura. When an image is stuck in your aura it constantly feeds you the same message. As you stay in the emotional state of whatever you are being fed by the charged picture you will tend to unconsciously and automatically keep feeding the charged image so it grows larger and takes over your conscious awareness. So, for example, if a spider picture got triggered and instead of returning to the filing system in your chakra, it got stuck permanently in your aura, you would start to see spiders everywhere and he afraid of spiders all of the time. You would see spiders where there are no spiders. You would overreact and be controlled by the stuck image.

When we teach clairvoyant skills, one of the very first skills we show people is how to de-energize mental image pictures. In this way you can always release a fear, get rid of a pain, de-energize a stuck emotion or pattern, so that nothing can remain stuck in your aura. This is one of the most wonderful clairvoyant skills that we teach as this skill allows you to shift your thought patterns, your feelings and emotions and your actions in life. Once you can see the aura and recognize an image you can choose to release it and create the life you want to have. You become the master of your own energy and the creator of your lifestyle. This is indeed a spiritual skill that can change your life.

Conflicts in your aura

A conflict is when you want to do or act on two different opposite concepts. You want to go to work but you are tired and need a vacation, so you also want to stay home and rest. You love two men but can only marry one of them. You need to do a project for work but you also want to go to the movie with a friend.

Whenever you have a choice where you have energy invested in both ends you have a conflict. Whenever you have a conflict your lost your motivation and your energy gets diffused. So even though you go to work though you really want to stay home or go on a vacation part of your energy stays at home energetically. Or part of your energy is just not focused and usable with you. If you meditate you will learn to be in the moment. When you view an aura you are in the moment or what we call Present Time. Every spiritual tradition will teach you to be in the moment. When you are in what we Clairvoyants call Present Time you are able to go beyond your conflicts and to focus all of your energy in one place at one time. Focusing all of your energy in one place at one time makes you powerful and successful in all that you do. It is in the NOW that you understand and know your past and create your future.

Conflicts slow your aura down and make it appear muddier. Conflicts cause confusion as you cannot make up your mind what to do and so you do whatever you are doing with less joy and less energy. If you become too conflicted and cannot make decisions you become paralyzed with indecision and confusion and then look to someone else to decide for you.

As you learn to see your aura you learn to know yourself and start to understand how to deal with your inner conflicts. Most of all you learn to recognize your hidden conflicts that lie beneath the surface and so clear yourself to create clear direct energy in your life.

Whenever you are afraid to take action or whenever you hesitate to do something in your life it is because a fear picture is lit up in your aura. This fear picture is also a conflict. You want to do something but you are afraid to change or afraid of whatever your fear is, so you have a conflict. Often when this happens you do nothing or take a much longer time to make a decision. Conflicts slow you down in life.

Fear or resistance to change

Often when you study or do something new you go into resistance. Your resistance to learning something new is actually your resistance to change. You know who you are now but once you learn a new skill you have to change and become a different person. You have to grow into the new you. People experience this when they study pottery, take a class in mathematics, learn a new language or study clairvoyancy. This is also what clairvoyants call "using effort." When you first study a new skill you will use more effort than you need to because the inner part of you will be in resistance to learning something new that can change your perceptions and identity.

Young children do not go into resistance when they learn a new skill. Adults do go into resistance because adults have a formed identity and are afraid of appearing awkward, unskilled, stupid, unable or just incapable of doing a new skill. And so adults will always take longer to learn something because we make it more difficult in the beginning stages of our learning process. Once we stop using effort and allow ourselves to believe we can do it we release the resistance to change and allow ourselves to integrate our new identity. If you try to learn to see the aura you might face your resistance of seeing "what most people think is invisible." Once you can view the aura you have taken your first step towards enlightenment. Seeing the aura allows you to know yourself and others, understand basic human behavior; open your awareness to higher levels of consciousness, and to take the first stepping-stone to enlightenment.

NEUROSIS OR STUCK ENERGY FROM CHILDHOOD

The two major areas where your energy gets stuck are stuck images from your past lives and emotions from your childhood.

Your past lives surface in an unconscious manner so usually you are not aware of this until you see a specific pattern that occurs over and over again. If you study meditation or clairvoyant techniques then you can learn to "see" the images of your past lives as they manifest in your aura. Most people only give weight to their past lives when they have a strong feeling of déjà vu.

Actual neurosis is when many images stay stuck in your aura and they get connected in a system so that the energy consistently moves through the images in the same order over and over again. So people who do this seem neurotic as they repeat their "stuckness'. They get stuck in a loop of their own energized pictures and cannot release themselves from this phenomenon. Usually psychiatrists give drugs to people who seem stuck in this manner. Therapists try to get the person to face one of their images and to combat it (release the charge it holds on them) as this will often cause a gap in their loop that will enable them to get beyond the loop phenomenon. Clairvoyants try to also get the person to release the energy in their pictures. Clairvoyancy can heal people with spiritual, emotional and physical problems by showing them how to release energy and to shift their consciousness. Clairvoyancy, however, cannot heal or cure true mental disease.

THE POWER OF HEALING

It is not a "gift" to see and heal the aura. It is the birthright, the ability given to each and every one of us when we are born. But to use this healing ability we have to wake up to our ability to empower ourselves with our inner knowledge. Some people do this naturally but most of us get cut off from our inner selves and need to involve ourselves in a spiritual study, some form of meditation or energy exercises to reawaken our true knowledge and abilities.

The knowledge of how to heal, to see clairvoyantly and to work with pure energy is stored within us. Our energy holds that key. And it is believed that this is also stored within the cellular DNA structure in our bodies. We have this information but we are born without the instruction manual of how to access it. Meditation or energy exercises open our awareness to accessing this both personal and universal level of knowledge and awareness. In almost all spiritual traditions there is some explanation that humans are either created in the image of God; or that humans have within them the ability to evolve into a god like or advanced state of being; or that all answers to the true reality is stored within us. This stored information is not just the personal answers of who you are, why you reincarnated in this body and what your purpose is in this life. It is selfish and shallow to look and just try to understand what your purpose is in this particular life. Stored within us is not just our particular personal information for one life but also the entire blueprint for humankind. Each person also has the information that eventually will allow all of us to understand the true nature of reality, the removing of the veil of ignorance that creates the physical world the way we view it today. The world, as we perceive it, is a shared agreement level. In other words, once enough people "wake up" to access the higher or true reality the world as we see it will shift and change to become a very different world.

In a religious sense people usually view the world as a divided one where there is a spiritual world and a physical world. When you die you leave the physical world behind and you enter the spiritual world. Many people tend to view the physical world as one filled with pain, fear and difficulty while they view the spiritual world as one of love, joy, immense beauty and shining immanence. But in truth it is all one world and there is no separation. There is a separation only because we believe and accept that separation. As you learn to clear your energy field, to still the mind, then you can vibrate at a totally different wavelength of energy. As you vibrate at a higher wavelength of energy you access a different field of the light and you create a different reality. It is not machines or Gods or anything outside of us that creates a different reality.

It is the human mind and consciousness that creates a different reality. This is becoming one with the universal spirit, transcending the mortal coil to everlasting life, or encountering the true unveiled reality.

As you learn to work with your energy, to move energy and to see instant change which we call "healing" you will come to realize and validate your true empowerment as a human being. Then and only then can we shift the current reality of pain, trauma, war, disease and hunger and move into a future that we create of our own inner desires.

There are many doorways to accessing the power of universal consciousness I have found clairvoyancy and energy healing to be one of those doorways. By learning to see energy you can view how it works and how you can change or shift it to create more of the reality you wish to have, By learning to move energy in the aura you learn how to heal or change yourself or another quickly and instantaneously. I will never forget the first time I did a healing when there was a tremendous and instantaneous change that not only "healed" the person I was working on but totally changed my life and consciousness in that very moment.

I had a friend who was prone to back aches. Her back would stiffen, then the muscles would lock up and she would be in tremendous pain. She had gone to doctors who could only offer her painkillers or muscle relaxants but could never find the cause of her malady. So therefore no doctor could tell her how to stop these back pains from happening. One day I suggested I try to do an energy healing. When healing both the aura and the energy body of a person, as a healer, you always try to shift the energy but at the same time you also look for the cause of the problem. If you can find the cause of the problem and get the person to release the cause then the problem will go away forever.

So I started healing my friend by creating some grounding for her so she could naturally release any stuck energies. Then I cleaned my friend's aura, removing any foreign energy and anything else she was ready to let go of. I further cleaned and balanced her energy centers (chakras) and the channels in her arms and legs. This is the basic Clearsight Energetic Medicine healing system I have been using and teaching since 1980. I started from the top of her head going downwards so that I would be bringing her energy focused into her body. This balanced and cleansed her basic energy. Then I searched for her back problem. It was easy to find since the lower part of her back was covered with a bright red energy. Red is the color of vibrancy but it is also the color of pain and heat. Where the pain was located it was covered with a bright red energy. I pulled the red energy out and de-energized it so I could see what was behind it. There I discovered a set of pictures that lined the bottom of her spine. These were past life pictures from when she was a man in the army in an Eastern European country riding a horse. When she rode for long hours her back would pain her. This picture would become energized or what we clairvoyants call lit up whenever she became tired or felt overworked or overloaded in life. Once this image flooded with energy and so became lit up like a stained glass window with sun flooding through it then her body would think this picture was her true reality. So her body, believing she had been riding a horse for many long hours, would pain her and then her muscles would tighten up and spasm and severe pain would start to plague her.

As I de-energized the past life horseback riding pictures and put them in her memory banks where they really belonged my friend let out a great sigh as the pain disappeared. I drained out the spasm energy from her muscles, relaxed her back using cool blue calming energy and spoke to her unconscious mind explaining that it needed to learn to relax when she seemed overloaded or over tired. I verbally explained to my friend how to recognize when she was getting overloaded and how to use different methods to relax herself to avoid these pictures lighting up again. But what really transformed me as a healer was watching the pain in her face just release instantaneously. Once you use your energy and ability to heal someone and see him shift immediately you come to understand the vast and incredible power of working with energy. It is just staggering to move a small piece of energy and suddenly see a person completely change. The pain left my friend. Her skin color changed. Her sense of who she was changed. It was like looking at a totally different person. One who was happy and healthy. It was truly amazing both to watch and to accomplish.

As you learn to train yourself to see clairvoyantly you can see many energy channels in the body. You can see the meridians that acupuncturists use to treat a person. You can see the energy channels along the spine. You can see the energy in the internal organs. You can see the energy in the energy body. You can see all of these energies moving throughout the body as a whole and this allows you to view a person's health condition. Thus you have the ability to see the problems, to diagnose what causes them and with the permission of the person you can often move or shift energy to create a healthier more balanced state. If you heal and change the energy of a person then the body, the physical, mental and emotional states will follow and start to heal or fix the problem. Our clairvoyant saying is always, "Energy First." Once you change the energy everything else realigns to follow the new pattern.

Healing a person using energy is easy to do. You do not have to have access to medicine, herbs, or tools. Just by shifting a person's energy you can make an incredible difference. Sometimes you can remove pain or cause diseases to disappear. Sometimes you can shift a person to a new level of consciousness where they can begin to heal themselves. It does not mean that you can always do a "miracle" healing. Sometimes you can shift a person's energy and that enables that person to then find the physical herb, medicine, exercise or answer to finishing the healing process. Once a person shifts their energy a new pattern starts that send them on the healing path to a different reality.

Healing is the act of creating change. All living things have an aura. The aura is not just simply the energy around the body but also the life force energy that the body radiates.

Healing is not just relegated to human beings. You can use energy to heal animals, or living creatures, plants, the environment and the earth itself. Once you can view the world as energy you can also learn to influence or move that energy to create a more balanced world. Several spiritual groups have experimented with taking an abandoned lot of dumping lot in the city and shifting the energy to find that once this is done someone will come along who creates a small park or uses the land in a constructive way for the community. Healing is a wondrous and powerful tool that anyone can practice if they choose to focus their energy in that way.

Chapter Six
Living In Color

The rainbows of your life: Living in color

Our world is full of colors which most of the time we take for granted. Many studies have been done about color, telling us that if you paint walls green in a hospital people will be more relaxed but if you paint the walls red in a restaurant the clients will spend less time eating. Now there are experts who can tell you "what colors you should wear to enhance your appearance" based on your skin color and the time of year you were born; or the time of year you are identified with. Color is an intrinsic part of our lives that we usually take for granted. The colors in your home, the colors you wear and the colors where you work do affect you both unconsciously and consciously.

However, the colors of your aura are different because the colors of your aura reflect what you are feeling and experiencing in your life at any given time. The colors of your aura are the real colors of your personal inner life. What you feel, both consciously and unconsciously, what you think and what actions you take are expressed as colors in your aura. If you can see a person's aura you can understand their actions and motivations. The person's aura is their soul taking action through their body in this life.

When you look at the aura you first see many fantastic swirling colors. A healthy aura is always moving. It can be mesmerizing and overwhelming to watch the aura. At Clearsight we have developed a system for being able to easily "read" the aura so that you can get information about a person's health, finances, love life or spirituality. Since the aura is a maze of swirling color we find it easier to read the aura layer by layer. When you read the aura by layer you can easily get information about specific areas of a person's life.

Perceiving Color

If you look directly at the aura it can be overwhelming to view. Many swirling colors moving around a person. Some of the colors are clear, bright and transparent while others are smoky, thick, chunky, thick, heavy and muddled. At Clearsight we developed a system for reading the aura layer by layer to make it easier to define and understand what you are seeing. The colors have texture, thin or thickness, clarity or cloudy condition, and bright or dull.

It is not always useful to read books that tell you what each color means because there are many variants of a particular color. If you walk into a paint store and look for one particular color you will usually find 30 or more paint swatches with samples of that color in varying degrees of lightness. When you read an aura each color is specific to the person you are reading. So the particular shade of green that the person you are reading has a very specific meaning to that person. You have to look carefully to assess what that color means to that person and not just what that color generally means. It can differ.

In an aura not all color is solid. If you are walking down the street in the city and see a person with what looks like a red aura he might be a very angry person or he might be a very energized person. One shade of bright red means anger.

Another, very similar shade of red, means the person is very energized. Some athletes have a very bright red in parts of their aura. A darker shade of red might mean the person stores old anger he has never released. As the color shifts the meaning shifts. If a person has a reddish brown or maroon color he might be very frustrated about something. If he has a reddish grey he might feel powerless in some situation and frustrated because of it. There are many variations in the aura and often these are particular or unique to the person you are viewing.

Often when people see red they think they are seeing a solid color. But usually what they are really seeing are drops of red sprinkled in one layer of the aura that then get reflected

Levanah Shell Bdolak

throughout the aura to look like a solid color. Red is often easy to notice because it is such a bright color.

As students of the aura learn to read in depth they come to understand how to see why a color is relevant to the person they are reading and what it means to that person. You do not learn to do this with your mind. You learn to do this with your energy self. Often when students learn to read the aura they suspend their mind, still their conscious thoughts and use their energy self to get their answers. This is the same process that people use when meditating. As you learn to still your mind you get more in touch with the divine nature of the energy universe. You integrate your lower personality nature in this life with your upper soul nature and so come into a space of oneness. It is this space of oneness that allows you to see and act as spirit. It is also this space of oneness that will eventually evolve you into your higher nature. If you learn to clear yourself while reading the aura then it is one way of accessing your divine nature. It can be a doorway to the next step in your personal evolution.

LIVING IN THE LIGHT

An aura is light. According to all spiritual traditions everything is made of the light.

Many energy workers believe that if you can see everything as light you will transcend to the next dimension. In the Buddhist tradition there are many dimensions, which often they call "heavens."

It is very rare to see a person whose aura is all one color. This is the mark of a holy person who has studied and practiced the same style of meditation or energy skills for many years. Often you will see Buddhist monks in Thailand who have a saffron color in the outer two layers of their auras (the religious and spiritual layers). But usually they do not have this saffron color in their entire aura. To have this saffron color throughout their whole aura they have to enter the basic enlightenment state that Buddha entered, to clear their energy of all desires and emotions. Few people do this. To surrender to spirit and yet be of the physical earth takes a certain type of consciousness. You have to be willing to "lose" everything to "gain" everything. Few people follow this path in our modern times.

THE AURA AS A SPHERE OF INFLUENCE

Whatever is in your aura is what you will create in your life. If your energy gets mixed up with someone else's energy and their energy is in your aura then you will start to create what that person wants in life. This can take you off your true path. Some young people go to the college or university their parents want them to attend. Others marry the person their family wants them to marry. Some people work in a family business because they feel indebted and pressured to do so.

Within your aura are patterns and programs. If these patterns or programs belong to a different person you will follow them as if they are your own. Free Will is the state of owning your energy and having only your own energy within your aura. Sometimes people pick up random energy by rubbing up against a person in a train or on a crowded bus but this is fairly rare. If you pick up energy in this manner you might get home and realize that you felt happy on the way home til suddenly you began to feel sad or angry or the effects of whatever energy you accidentally picked up. When a particular emotional energy enters your aura it then begins to light up the images of your own sad or angry or similar energy that you hold and so can affect you. But usually this effect will wear off in a few hours. If you are consciously aware of your basic emotional state you will notice that something has shifted you and you will release or de-energize the energy that shifted you and shift out of your triggered emotional state.

More often people are affected by programs from friends and family who want them to live their life in a certain manner. Sometimes parents want a child to be successful in the same career path that they are in and so program the child. We call this the "Be a doctor" syndrome. The parents want the child to follow in their footsteps or to be in a high earning stable career, such as medicine; and so they send energy into that person's aura or energy centers (chakras) to create this. Programming is often done unconsciously by the parents. As you read an aura you can see patterns and programs quite clearly. I have seen beginning readers notice this though they often do not understand what they are seeing. A program appears as a design that is set and does not move. Sometimes it is repeated throughout the aura. Sometimes it is just in one area of the aura. When a clairvoyant sees energy that belongs to someone else in a person's aura they simply return it to where it came from.

Free Will is very important. You can here to live out your own chosen path of learning and experience. You did not incarnate to fulfill your parents, friends or spouse's dreams. You incarnated to carry out your own evolutionary purpose. It is imperative that you live your life freely to do this. Otherwise you are wasting your time in this body and will simply have to repeat the learning you do not accomplish in your next life!

Some people do not realize that they do not have Free Will until they get a healing or reading and have their aura cleared. Suddenly they feel whole or in touch with their true nature, happy and more at peace within themselves. When you are severely influenced by someone else's needs it creates a conflict within you that often creates a smoldering level of anger on an unconscious level. This "hidden" anger often causes health problems and some levels of dysfunction in every day daily life. When this gets released a person feels free and joyous and more in touch with their inner self.

HOW COLOR APPEARS

Color in an aura is not stable. It changes constantly. If you tell someone you love them and they also love you their aura will change in places to a rose, pink or peach color, the colors of love. If you listen to a lecture your aura will have some bright yellow in it. If you see something that you are afraid of part of your aura will turn bright red or reddish grey. If you become sad about the loss of a friend your aura will turn dark blue. If you become depressed your aura will turn an even darker blue. All of this is changeable. Your emotional mood and what you react to is constantly changing. Most people do not understand or know how to truly control their emotions or awareness so their auras constantly change as they flit from one feeling to another. People who meditate daily or study a meditative spiritual tradition learn to assess, know and control their emotions through a form of conscious awareness and meditative practice or use of energy skills.

THE LAYERS OF THE AURA

Your aura is a creation of all of the energy of your past, your present and your future. It is the book of your life and in doing so is also the colors of your life. There are seven basic layers in an aura. The seven layers correspond to the seven energy centers (chakras) that are aligned along your spine. As the energy moves through your system it moves through the chakra and into the corresponding layer of your aura. By reading the layers of an aura you can know and tell a great deal about a person. Each layer also has seven layers within it but usually when a clairvoyant reads the aura they mostly only read one or two layers in each layer.

The following is a basic description of each layer and what type of information you can glean from reading it.

FIRST LAYER
LETS GET PHYSICAL

The first layer of your aura is the physical layer. It is the energy directly around your body. It shows you about a person's health, his relationship to his body, his comfort level about where he is located, and his physical strength, activity and well being.

SECOND LAYER
I AM WHAT I FEEL

The second layer of your aura is the emotional, sensual and sexual layer. It is the layer of how you feel about things,

THIRD LAYER
I AM WHAT I DO

The third layer of your aura governs thought into action. Here is the information of what you actually do in the physical world: your job, your activities, your hobbies, your movement, and your actions.

FOURTH LAYER
LOVE IS THE TRUE CONNECTION

The fourth layer of your aura is your identity. It shows your self-esteem, your ability to love yourself and others and your ability to connect to be one with the universal energy source. It is your personality in <u>this</u> life.

FIFTH LAYER
COMMUNICATION

Your fifth layer is your communication layer. It holds all of the information about how you communicate. The fifth layer often holds past lives and future lives for you to see and know.

SIXTH LAYER
SPIRITUAL: WHAT GIVES MEANING TO YOU

The sixth layer of your aura is your clairvoyant layer. Here you have the ability to see. This is considered your spiritual layer as it determines what gives meaning to your life.

SEVENTH LAYER
RELIGION AND HIGHER KNOWLEDGE

The seventh layer of your aura is the layer of wisdom, religion and higher knowledge. Here you can see what a person is bringing in for their future, what their Higher Self believes and acts upon and what religions govern them in their actions.

THE COLORS OF THE AURA

Color is a vibration. It ranges from light to dark, thick to thin, heavy to light and dull to bright. Your aura is your personal universe. The colors within it mirror what is happening to you at the moment.

WHITE

White is not a color. However, all of the colors are contained within white. White is the highest vibration. Usually it is too high to run or keep in a body so we use gold, which is the highest vibration that the body can use and absorb. White protects the body, the aura, the Higher Self and the Soul. When a person is frightened he will naturally and unconsciously bring white light into his aura to protect himself. When he feels safe the white light will release and disappear. White light is like snow. It tends to freeze the aura. If you want to grow fast do not use white light. Use gold light. White protects you but it freezes your development at exactly where you are right now. If you put too much white light in your aura many Beings will look at you and tend to surround you. White light is very bright and tends to attract many out of body Beings.

MILKY WHITE

Milky white is the color that fills your aura when you are sick and lie on your back in a hospital bed for many months. Milky white is the color of long-term illness.

LIGHT YELLOW

Light Yellow is an active color that is in the aura of athletes and physically active people.

Bright yellow

Bright yellow is the color of the intellect. You will see this color around the head of professors and lecturers and people who think a lot.

Kelley green

Kelley Green is the color of growth, of spring growth and of change.

Forest green

Forest Green, the deep green color, is the color of a soul healer. It is also the color of deep emotional growth and transformation. If you have a lot of Forest Deep Green you are a spiritual healer and a person who has deep transformative change and can affect all around you to change also.

Avocado green

Avocado Green is the color of envy, greed and envious desire.

Lime green

This is the color of a person with a gentle nature who changes easily.

Sea green

Sea Green is the color of an easygoing person who is relaxed and goes with the flow or changes easily. People who have a lot of sea green in their aura usually have studied meditation in past lives or grown up or lived near the sea. They are very relaxed people!

Orange red

Orange-Red is the color of deep vibrant strong energy. People who have orange-red color in their aura can be powerful healers. Orange-red can be a positive energy but it also can be a negative energy as it can also represent unresolved emotions and out of control feelings. Orange-red is a powerful energy. If used powerfully it is the energy of passionate change. If used negatively it is the energy of stubborn holding on to heavy old emotions. Powerful healers have orange, orange-red and deep forest green in their auras.

Red

Red is the color of vitality. Positively bright red color in your aura means you are strong, vital, healthy and full of energy. Negatively, red in your aura means you are an angry person with unresolved conflicts. Red auras are usually people who are easily triggered into anger. But bright red auras of athletes are the auras of very energetic people. A person who runs in a race of bicycles in a race has a lot of bright red color in his aura.

SCARLET

Scarlet is an orange red color that indicates a very outgoing social person.

BURGUNDY

Burgundy is the color of a perfectionist and usually a very conservative person.

MALAGRA

If you aura is the color of malagra wine you are a very passionate person.

BRICK RED

Brick Red is the color of frustration.

MAROON

When the aura has a dark maroon color it tells us that thus person is a very stubborn person.

FUCHSIA

Fuchsia color in the body layers of the aura (layers one through four) is the color of feminine creativity and feminine love of beauty. Fuchsia in the sixth and seventh layers of the aura is the color of spiritual love. Many Buddhists in Thailand have fuchsia in the seventh layers of their auras.

MAGENTA

Magenta is a strong feminine color.

PEACH

Peach is the color of mother love, of father love and of nurturing love. You will often see peach color in the auras of nurses and in the aura of mothers and fathers who have young babies.

PINK

Pink is the color of young love.

ROSE

Rose color is the color of love in the aura. When a couple gets married you will see rose in their auras.

CANDY PINK

Practicing socially acceptable behavior mannerisms.

MELON

Melon in the aura shows gentle nurturing energy.

LIGHT APRICOT

Gentle energy but sometimes not owning your power or seniority. Light apricot is often seen in the aura of people who join cults or non Free Will Religions or rhetorical groups.

BEIGE

Beige is the color of non-ownership. Cult followers often have some beige in every layer of their aura. A person with a lot of beige in his aura does not control his own reality and lets others make decisions for him.

BROWN

Brown is an earthy color. It gives solidity to a person but too much it makes a person slow, heavy and dull. Farmers and people who live close to the earth often have a lot of brown in their first two layers of the aura, the physical and emotional layers. If a person has brown in the third or fourth layers, the layers of action and identity then the person is very earthy but also probably stable but very slow and heavy in taking action or making decisions.

DARK BROWN

Dark Brown is a heavy color that means a person moves slowly. Slow, deliberate and ponderous movement is indicated when a person has dark brown. People who are impoverished, whose main activity is in finding food to eat or tribal people who hunt and gather often have dark brown around their bodies and in their fourth layers. Dark Brown means a person has a strong survival connection with the earth. Often these people who have dark brown in their fourth and fifth layers are slow communicators who do not use verbal skills but tend to use their bodies more. Ancient peoples tended to use the lower chakras more for survival. In more modern times we are evolving into using the higher energy centers more and so use higher and lighter colors. Dark Brown is truly a color of living on the land in the ancient manner.

LIGHT SKY BLUE

Sky blue is a very spiritual color but usually when you see it in a person's aura it means that person is spacey, ungrounded and does not get to appointments on time!

BRIGHT BLUE

Bright blue or what we commonly call "gas flame blue" signifies that the person is very psychic.

TURQUOISE

Turquoise is the color of abundance. If you see this is someone's fifth layer they are good at creating whatever they want and need.

Blue green

Blue-Green is the color of fluid change. People who have this color in their aura are easy going, relaxed, good therapists, good listeners and often people who grew up at the beach or live at the seaside. People with blue-green in their aura often had past lives where they studied meditation or yoga.

Cobalt blue

Cobalt Blue is the color of both personal, traditional and national morality. You will see cobalt blue in the auras of policemen, soldiers, security personnel, judges, lawyers and authority figures. Cobalt Blue is the color of right and wrong, strong beliefs and fixed moral beliefs.

Lavender

Lavender is the color of present time spirituality. You will see this in the aura of New Age or metaphysical people people who want to express their spirituality in their lives now.

Purple

Purple is the auric color of religion and intensity. If there is purple in someone's aura that person is intense. He may have been very religious in a past life or very religious now or simply very intense and dedicated to whatever he does.

VIOLET

Violet is a very spiritual and inspirational color.

RED VIOLET

Red violet is the color of karma. When you see this in a person's aura they have a lot of karma to work out with people in this life. People who were kings or queens, rulers or leaders in past lives often bring in their unfinished karma to this life to complete and often have red violet in the outer three layers of their aura (layers 5, 6 & 7). Musicians, performers, actors, actresses and politicians and all people who are in the public eye are usually working out karma from past lives. This means they still feel responsible to either help, teach or share information with people.

INDIGO

Indigo is the color of the new intuitive Beings incarnating onto our planet. Indigo is a deeply intuitive, spiritual and newly innovative color.

GREY

Grey is the color you get when silver, the color of power, sinks, and you doubt your own capability. Grey is the color that tells you a person is stuck.

GREY-RED

Grey-Red is the color of fear.

Grey-brown

Grey-Brown is the color of difficult survival. Whenever you see grey it means that a person is using a lot of effort to accomplish whatever they are doing. Grey-Brown means that a person is usually living a life in struggle, difficulty and survival. Often these are people who live on the land hunting and gathering or in poverty in difficult situations.

Silver

Silver is the color of power and of personal empowerment.

Gold

Gold is the highest color (energy) you can put in your aura that is compatible with the human body and will allow you to remain fluid and adaptable. Gold is the color of the sun, and of success.

Black

Black is not a color. It is the lack of color. If you see black in someone's aura it means they are missing some of their information.

Seeing in color

Whenever I do a public appearance where I speak about the aura I also encounter that many people seem to think seeing the aura is a special and very unusual ability. But to the contrary, seeing in color is what we as Energy Beings are able to do naturally. If you study for less than five months you can begin to open yourself to the easy ability to see the colors of the aura.

Your Higher Self sees the aura whenever it looks at a person. So once you make a good connection with your Higher Self you can also see and get this information. Thus seeing the aura is a natural skill that you are born with.

Many years ago I was scheduled to give a Healing Seminar in Kansas. The local New Age TV Program set up an evening for me to explain to people how energy healing works. About sixty people showed up for my talk. I spoke about energetic medicine, healing the aura and the chakras. In the beginning of my talk I asked the audience how many people could see an aura. Two people raised their hands. These were the two people who were representatives of the New Age TV program.

After my talk about twelve people came up to the podium to speak with me. And they said, "It was difficult to listen to you." I felt I had spoken simply and covered the topic in a way that anyone could understand it. And so I was shocked at this statement, and so I asked them why it was so difficult to listen to me speak. And they answered, "There was this very beautiful green energy that kept flowing out of your hands and we were watching that."

My response was, "I thought you guys told me that you do not see auras!" And they answered back, "Oh we don't see auras. But that sure was a beautiful light show of green energy that kept moving out of your hands!" And once again I was shocked. "But you were seeing my healing energy and that is just the same as seeing an aura!" And once again the twelve people all nodded in unison and answered that they don't see auras.

Often people do not know what an aura is and when they see it or see colorful energy moving they do not identify it as *seeing an aura*. In modern culture we are not given any permission to "see an aura" or even to discuss this when we do see an aura. It is something many people do not speak about in public. As I traveled around the United States doing speeches and presentations I have noticed an interesting phenomenon. At the end of the presentation there will always be some people who will come to speak with me privately. They often tell me their psychic, clairvoyant or intuitive experiences. And always they tell me that they never discuss this with their family or friends. Sometimes they tell me that "my family would not understand." Or, "they would think me strange." And so people tell me, the stranger, they have seen the aura or had a special energy experience because I have told them it is OK to speak about this.

CHAPTER SEVEN
SEEING IS BELIEVING

ANYONE CAN SEE AN AURA

Knowing that an aura has colors, pictures and layers does not help you to see and read the aura. People naturally begin to see the aura when their energy rises to a higher level and they spiritually open up to a new level of awareness. You can choose to shift your energy by doing different systems of meditation or energy work. If you would like to change your level of energy to see auras you can take a Clearsight class to learn the system that will raise your energy level and shift your awareness enough to see an aura. Or you can get my Six Step book, which has the very beginning exercises that will lead you to opening your third eye. It usually takes three or more months for these exercises to work for you if you use them consistently every day. To learn to actually read the aura I have always suggested that you study in a clairvoyant school, as you will go through many personal changes of awareness as you develop your higher nature.

Seeing the aura is the first step in individual evolution.

Evolving as spirit

We are very lucky to live in the twenty-first century. At this point in time you can learn meditation, develop your inner sight and trod the age old path of inner wisdom without having to be a hermit living in a cave or monastery on the mountain. You can have a family, go to work to earn a living and participate in your community and still, at the same time, develop your energy abilities. In the past you either had to dedicate your entire life to being a monk or nun or wait til your family grew up and you retired and then you could enter a monastery to pursue your spiritual life. Now you can do this and everything else too.

In Clairvoyant terms we define spirituality as that which gives you meaning in life. It is the skills of spirituality that show you what your true purpose is and the easiest way to accomplish it in this life. These skills and abilities can make your life easier, more joyous and can add immeasurable wisdom to your existence. And as you personally evolve it enables you to be a shining light for your family, your community and the human race. Every person who raises their vibration and acts out of their pure loving spirit helps to evolve the entire human race.

Often people come to me for Readings and they always ask what their path or purpose is in this life. There are several purposes or reasons we take a body. We reincarnate in a body to finish up old karma. These are the scenarios where we have retained some guilt or reason why we feel unfinished with a particular person and need to fix the situation in the next life. We also reincarnate to learn lessons. If we were unbalanced, acting selfishly or angrily we return to learn how to deal with that emotion in a better way. But we also return for reasons beyond our personal self. We have many agendas. Some of our higher vibration agendas involve helping the human race to advance itself.

As you open yourself to a higher vibration and you can see the aura, you will also start to access your past lives, your higher knowledge and your inner intuition. Seeing the aura leads you to the road of enlightenment. This leads you to the many spiritual levels of awareness often called the many heavens by Buddhist practitioners. As you climb the path of awareness you will recognize the spiritual energies that you originally come from and eventually return to.

FROM THE BEGINNING TO THE ENDING

This life is not your only life. Most people on this planet have had more than three hundred past lives. Usually people come to this planet and see that it has such a wonderful beauty and variety. They decide to stay here for one life and to learn something. But in that first life they usually create some type of karma and so wind up staying on and on to clear their karma and learn their lessons. As you move from life to life you learn about emotions, compassion, integrity, love and hate, good and bad. As you get to the end of one life you have learned a lesson and accumulated a certain amount of wisdom. That wisdom travels on with you to the next body but often it is hidden, only to emerge when it is needed. As you enter each new body you forget what came before. But your wisdom and learned experiences are there and can be accessed as you learn to get more in touch with your energy, your spiritual self. It is similar the way modern computers work. Often a person decides that he wants to sell his old computer so he erases his personal information. But a skilled computer expert will tell you that the information is still on the computer and can be accessed if you know the proper code. So the information seems gone and invisible but if you know how to access the computer properly you can pull it back. And so if you learn to meditate or enter the energy world you can access the important information from your past lives too.

And so each life you have is like a chapter in a book, or an accomplished goal along the obstacle course. Every ending is a beginning. Every beginning leads you to the ending. Your spirit does not die, it simply transforms.

FROM PHYSICAL TO SPIRIT---PASSING ON

Taking a body is a very fascinating experience. Everyone cheers and celebrates when a baby is born. People think that the baby is a blank screen but actually that baby carries with it all of the imprints and memories of past lives that have affected it strongly enough to be remembered. These memories are right below the mind's conscious level but strong enough to often affect the emotional body. This causes the child to act in reaction to it's past. Therefore the child carries both love and grief, positive and negative patterns and emotions he is not aware of. So the child has come to work out many old problems, issues and patterns to learn a better way.

We celebrate the child coming to be among us but actually we should reverse the process of celebration. The child comes to earth as an earth school of learning. Life can be fun and joyous but it will also have pitfalls of difficulties as this child meets his obstacles.

On the other hand, when an elder is ready to leave his body he has finished his learning in this life. He has accomplished some of his agenda. Maybe if he has been really focused he has accomplished most or all of his agenda. This truly is the time to celebrate. Now when the elder leaves he is ready to go on to a higher calling of his spirit. But of course, we humans will miss him. And so we grieve and want him to stay and so see his leaving as sadness and a loss. But actually going back to pure spirit is a very beautiful experience for the person who is leaving. Now he has put behind him the responsibilities of this

life and he is ready to move on to the spirit world where
there is time without ending or beginning; space without
boundary; life without effort; the potentate divinity of all
spirit; life everlasting; and the eternal creative life force
that is the Oneness.

When my husband's uncle died I got a call from my
mother-in-law. My mother-in-law hated to go to funerals
so she asked me to attend as her representative. My
husband groaned and rolled his eyes. He felt his mother
should attend the funeral out of respect but his mother
had quite a dislike for funerals. My mother-in-law was
a very warm and loving person and it was easy for me
to agree to stand in for her. After all, I hardly knew my
husband's uncle so I had little grief. This made the entire
situation easier for me.

On the day of the funeral we dressed in black, attended
the funeral Requiem and then proceeded to the gravesite
for the internment. Once at the gravesite it seemed like a
scene out of a bad movie. Everyone started to cry. Many
people did not want to cry in public so they tried to hold it
in and turned their heads downcast to the ground to hide
their eyes. Since I was not really attached to the deceased,
as I hardly knew him, I was not mourning in this manner.
And this gave me a chance to observe what was happening
energetically. The people who were grieving had brown,
blue and grey tinged auras. They looked depressed (blue),
aware of his body being returned to the earth (brown) and
felt powerless (grey) since people pass on no matter how
much we wish for them to stay on with us.

My husband's uncle was in his late sixties when he passed on. Suddenly the family had discovered he had Alzheimer's and within a very short year he progressed from a self-assured intelligent man to a lost soul who could not remember anything. It was definitely difficult for his wife and grown up children, as he suddenly could not remember who they were or even who he was. I could see at the funeral site that his family had images in their auras, remembering him, as he had been, strong and smart and a gentle loving man. But they grieved for their loss and a dark blue crushed their auras with its heavy intensity.

Standing on the side was my husband's uncle's Being. He was there and he was incredibly happy. He had dropped his body and was no longer wandering lost. He seemed to be observing all of his loved ones. He was happy and joyous because he had accomplished his mission and he was moving on. And somehow someone should have been celebrating his accomplishment. But everyone was grieving for their loss and no one but I saw his gentle soul standing there. And so is the realm of the human experience. We celebrate the birth of the baby who is just starting the school of human awareness but when that baby is grown and has finished its learning and is ready to leave we do not celebrate its accomplishment because we humans do not watch the energy and we are just to caught up in our lower emotions of loss and grief. You might say it is only natural to grieve and there is a truth in that. But if you can see your relative standing there, at the graduation of his life learning, you will also see a joy and happiness of accomplishment that does not engender grief. Seeing the aura, seeing the spirit or soul, opens you to understanding the process of life and the awareness of spirit. This changes you forever. It allows you the ability to see beyond the stuck human condition and to grasp the wings of heaven and to fly in your consciousness.

I end this book with the saying we use at our Clearsight Clairvoyant School:

"If that which thou seekest
thou findest not within thee
Thou wilt never find it without thee."

Appendix
Learning To See The Aura

I have to tell you honestly that it is best to study to see the aura in a classroom situation. It is easy to learn to see an aura. Most people can do that within three to five months in our Clairvoyant Program. But it takes longer to understand what you are seeing and what it really means. That takes learning to access your intuitive insight. It is much easier to study to see an aura in a classroom atmosphere where you are given permission and aided in finding your way. I studied alone for many years and I discovered that it was very easy to get lost or side tracked along the way. Seeing the aura is easy but understanding the import of your sight and how to use the knowledge to help and aid others takes time and experience.

Once you can see an aura easily and clearly you are a resource, both to yourself and others. Seeing the aura is only the beginning of your evolution. Once you can see energy you can also move it to change your life and to shift your perspective. Change is another word for healing. If you can "see" the aura you can see illness as it starts to manifest and you can dissolve, move or shift it into healing before it even takes hold in the body. You can see the truth from the lie, the inner motivations of others and the beauty of love and joy that fills some people. You can also see the restrictions that stop you from experiencing that love and joy and once seeing these, you can de-energize or remove them and in so doing change your life significantly. By seeing the aura you become the architect of your life, the master of your dreams and the creator of your path.

Seeing the aura is one of the most fun paths that leads you to inner awareness and enlightenment. It teaches you to shift from sadness to joy, from depression to inspiration, from boring to exciting, and from wandering aimlessly to inner self- identity. Seeing the aura is a true path of evolutionary consciousness.

An Introduction To Inner Sight

Inner sight is the true sight. Your inner awareness will tell you what is actually happening and why. You can learn to understand the past, take action in the present and create the kind of future you want to have.

Skills To See With

The skills in this appendix are the basic skills we show people who want to become clairvoyant and evolve into a higher level of awareness. By learning the skills of Grounding, Center of the Head, Running Energy and De-Energizing Mental Image Pictures you allow yourself to clear your life force energy in a very quick dramatic and fun loving manner.

Grounding enables you to feel safe and secure, to heal your body and to allow yourself to change and grow in consciousness and action. Center of the Head allows you to bring your Higher Self into your body so that you can see auras, access a higher level of information and know what you came here to do in this life. Running Energy is basically taking an "energy shower." It clears other people's energy anything old that you do not need anymore from your aura and your energy centers. Most people see the aura and colors if they run energy for three or four months consistently. Running Energy makes you feel clean from the inside of you. De-Energizing Mental Image Pictures allows you to release the charged energy from old trauma, patterns, memories, past lives and current life experience. It allows you to come into present time and to clear your energy so that you can see clearly.

Skills That Can Change Your Life

Grounding

Grounding is the one skill that can make you into an incredibly evolved human being, a super fine clairvoyant, a well balanced person, and strong focused, functional, and successful at whatever you do. In olden times people did not need grounding because they lived on the land and were always in touch with their bodies and the natural cycles of the earth. Nowadays most of us live in the cities and we are using our higher energy centers to think conceptually and are less in touch with the earth energies. We often do not naturally exercise and sometimes even have to schedule time to be in the garden.

The style of grounding that has been taught in many modern New Age metaphysical groups since the early 70's has been to create roots from your feet, like a tree, that goes down into the earth. We Clairvoyants have discovered that this type and style of grounding is not strong enough to ground your entire system. All of your powerful energy centers – the chakras that govern who you are in this life – are located in the center of your body along your spine. To properly ground them and release excess energy and have strong centering we use the new modern process of grounding from the First Chakra. This enables the entire body system to be grounded powerfully and directly.

Once you are grounded your entire system functions as one unit to focus all of your energy into whatever you choose to do at the moment. This is one of the key secrets of being a good clairvoyant, as you need to put your full focus into what you are doing. Most modern people are scattered having their energies interested in to many things at once. You may be interested in many ways of using your energy but you can only do one thing at one time. As you learn to ground you will notice that you will stop losing and forgetting things. If you lose something you will know how to quickly find it. You will discover that grounding enables you to be more centered and focused in your life and that your sense of self will automatically be more powerful.

Grounding brings all of your energy and your focus into one place and that is channeling your own life force energy through your body. Many spiritual systems promise their followers that they will become powerful individuals who can create their own realities. But most of these systems only work partially. Grounding makes you more powerful at whatever you do because it focuses all of your energy directly through your body in present time. Once you can do this you can create whatever you want and need in this life on a practical level because you are truly here to do it.

How to Ground

Find yourself a chair that is comfortable and has a straight back. Take off your shoes so you can make a connection with the earth. Sit in the chair and make sure that your feet touch the ground fully. Sit up straight but not stiffly. Close your eyes and take a nice deep breath and just say hello to yourself. If anyone else says hello back to you send them home. This time is just for you. This is your time to get in touch with your own Inner Self so if you keep thinking about someone else send them home.

At the base of the spine in men and a little further forward between your ovaries in women is an energy center we call the First or Root Chakra. Chakra is a Sanskrit word. It has many meanings but simply it means a wheel that spins. Your chakra is a vortex of energy that is shaped like a cone and is wide in the front and narrowed to a cone in the back. It goes through your body and is your energy machinery. So your chakra is a spiral cone of energy. All of your body chakras are situated sideways- with the wide part of the cone in the front of your body and the narrow part in the back of your body. From your Crown upwards, the energy centers (chakras) above your head are situated like a crown with the wide part of the cone on the bottom.

Be aware of your First Chakra but do not put your consciousness in it. Your First Chakra governs food, clothing, shelter and survival. If you put your energy into your First Chakra you will go into the survival mode and think about paying your bills. This is not comfortable. So do not put your energy or your consciousness into your First Chakra. Just become aware of your First Chakra.

Take some energy from your First Chakra and send it down through the chair, through the floor, through the earth, all the way down to the center of the earth. This is your Grounding Cord. It can be like a tree with roots that goes down to the center of the earth and hooks on. It can be like a beam of light that goes down to the center of the earth and surrounds it. It can be like a chain with an anchor that hooks into the center of the earth. It can be like a cat's tail that goes down to the center of the earth and encircles it. Whatever works for you! Send your grounding cord from your First Chakra down through the chair, through the floor, through the earth, all the way down to the center of the earth and hook it on. This is your grounding cord.

As your grounding hooks into the center of the earth it supports you. Now the earth is holding you up. If you have any tension in your body or anything that makes you feel uncomfortable send it down your grounding cord, all the way down to the center of the earth. When it gets to the center of the earth it will get released and come back to you as new life force energy.

If you find something that will not go down your Grounding Cord do not worry. I will cover another skill that will also show you how to release anything you are ready to let go of.

You can be grounded anywhere and all of the time. From the moment you wake up you will want to put down a Grounding Cord and use it all day long. If you put a Grounding Cord down early in the morning you will find that you wake up sooner, feel more refreshed and more alert in your body.

You can be grounded while you are on a train or walk around and you will discover that you function better at whatever you do. Your Grounding Cord moves with you.

Grounding makes your body feel safe, real, loved and it enables you to easily bring your Higher Self into your body. This newer form of Grounding with a cord of energy directly from your First Chakra enables you to ground your entire energy system fully. The old method of grounding with roots from your foot chakras really only secures the energy in your legs. But the real powerful dynamic energy in your body is in the chakras (the energy centers) along your spine. As you ground from your First Chakra you allow all of the energy from the entire system to balance and drain off excess. As you ground your Higher Self enters your body and realigns with it.

Creating A Higher Consciousness

There is a part of your consciousness that is the essence of your spirit. It is the part of you that creates your destiny, chooses your actions, and is always in touch with the wholeness of nature or the oneness of the universe. If you connect with this part of yourself then you have access to a tremendous amount of information about yourself and everything around you. The Romans called this your genius. The Greeks called it your daimon. The Christians called it your guardian angel. (Many researchers have discovered that what modern people call the guardian angel nowadays was actually in the past a reference to the Higher Self. Later it became fashionable to see this as a separate angel that "looks over you.") Plato called it your paradeigma. The Neoplatonists called it your ochemal (your imaginal body). The Egyptians referred to it as your ka or ba with which you could converse. Some Shamans referred to it as your spirit. Others called it your free-soul, animal soul, or breath-soul. Some called it your soul-image. New Agers refer to it as your Higher Self. And Clairvoyants also call it your Higher Self or your Spiritual Being.

As you learn to bring the essence of your Higher Self into your body you will begin to be able to communicate with it on a daily basis. When you bring the Higher Self into the body it is your Higher Essence that almost automatically heals you. It looks at you and sees what is not balanced and it rebalances it for you. Basically, all you have to do is to bring in your Higher Essence into your body and it starts to heal and rebalance you and to also give you information. If you stay grounded then you "hear" the information and can use it.

Center of your head

Once you have grounded yourself you will want to bring your consciousness, which is the lower aspect of your Higher Self into your body. Once you decide to bring in your higher essence into your body you have to choose where in your body you will bring your spirit. The most neutral place to bring your spiritual self into is what we Clairvoyants call the Center of Your Head. The Center of your Head is in your head but it is not your mind. It is an empty space right in the middle of your head. This

119

is bilaterally balanced and is an empty space that Mother Nature created just for your spiritual self to sit in.

To do this you will want to understand where the Center of your Head is located.

This is an easy exercise for finding the Center of Your Head. Take your hands and place them at about an inch from the top of your ears and point inwards and draw an imaginary line across your head from one hand to the other - or from the top of one ear to the other. Put one hand in front of you at the middle of your forehead and place the other hand directly behind you at the back of your head and draw another imaginary line through your head. Where the two lines intersect is the actual Center of Your Head. Now, be IN the Center of Your Head. Yes, just take a deep breath, close your eyes and place your entire consciousness in the Center of Your Head.

Take a good look around in the Center of Your Head. This should be an empty space! And it should belong to you and you alone! Whoever is in the area we call the Center of The Head is able to consciously control your entire body.

From the Center of Your Head you can receive all of your spiritual information as it comes down into the body and also neutrally receive all of your body information. As your spiritual self sits in the Center of Your Head you can "feel" your body as well as "knowing" your intuitive, psychic and transformational information. Turn on all of the lights in the Center of Your Head and view your space.

Is there anyone else in there with you? Often you will find a friend, relative, parent or child sitting in the Center of Your Head. And if you do find someone, say hello to them and send them back to their bodies. If someone sits in the center of your head and thinks about eating a chocolate candy bar your body will want a chocolate candy bar. So if you see anyone in the Center of Your Head send them back to their own bodies.

If you are looking at yourself sitting in the center of your head or if you are looking AT the Center of Your Head then you are not sitting IN the Center of Your Head. Make sure you are sitting directly in the Center of Your Head and not viewing it like looking into the window of a candy shop.

Please do not confuse the Center of Your Head with your Mind! The Center of Your Head is a very neutral space where you can place your Higher Being's consciousness and experience peace and that incredible spiritual oneness. The analytical Mind is your brain computer that enables you to process information and make rational judgments. The Mind enables you to analyze a situation. Being in the Center of Your Head allows you to use all of your higher intuitional ability to be still and know what works for you.

Bring a large golden sun above your head and let it come down into the Center of Your Head and as it fills the Center of Your Head with its radiant energy own the Center of Your Head and bring it into Present Time.

Present Time is being in the moment in the here and now.

Sitting in the Center of Your Head could be likened to sitting in the cockpit of the plane so that you can SEE your voyage in life clearly or to sitting in the best seat at the movie theatre.

If you are placing your consciousness directly in the Center of Your Head you might see a bright golden light. We call this light, enlightenment. Do not worry if you do not see this light. I am just telling you just in case you do see it.

When people walk through life grounded and in the Center of their Heads they walk with gracefulness, bearing and purpose because they are moving from their internal center. As you walk through life grounded and in the center of your head you are bringing your consciousness INTO the body and you will begin to walk as one with your Higher Self and just instantaneously know what is happening for you. Walking grounded and in the Center of Your Head is like having gone to psychic charm school because it totally changes your bearing, your balance and your image- like making you into a King or a Queen.

Now, be in the Center of Your Head and create a little trap door in the bottom of the Center of Your Head. Create an energy broom or vacuum cleaner and clean out the center of your head. Sometimes you will find dirt and dust here, sometimes filling cabinets, sometimes garbage and wine bottles left over from a party. Clean up the center of your head and sweep or dump it all down the trap door. It will go down the trap door and into your grounding cord and get released into the center of the earth and either come back to you as new life force energy or go back to wherever it belongs. The Center of Your Head should be a well-lit clean empty space just for you and you alone.

Create a sofa or chair for yourself and put it directly in the Center of Your Head so that you can sit there and look out the front as if you are looking out the front picture window of your home.

Some people discover the Center of Their Head quite easily and find it to be comfortable. Others have never been there and need time to adjust to having the wonderful new ability of being able to sit back and SEE clearly from the best seat in the house.

From the Center of Your Head you do not have to think, listen, weigh, judge, consider or feel---you can just be one with yourself and with the universe.

When you are in the Center of Your Head it is very easy to know things and to see the aura.

Running energy

Running Energy is a meditation and also an altered state of consciousness. It is a way of simply and easily changing your energy and the quality of your life. Running Energy is like taking an energy shower. It washes or pushes away all of the old and unwanted energy and cleans every cell, channel and chakra in your body. The process of

Running Energy naturally moves everyone else's energy out of your body and energy system.

To Run Energy you have to first be grounded and in the Center of Your Head.

Put a grounding cord down. Send some energy from your first chakra down to the center of the earth to create your grounding cord and hook it in and Be in the Center of Your Head.

At the bottoms of your feet, in the souls of your feet, are energy centers called foot chakras. They open and close like the lens of a camera or the iris of an eye. Be aware of your foot chakras and open them up to a place that seems comfortable for you and conceptualize bringing up about 15% earth energy through your feet, up your legs, through your thighs, into your First Chakra and down your grounding cord. Now keep that energy running. You are bringing up 15% earth energy up your foot chakras and up the channels in your legs, all the way up into your First Chakra and down your grounding cord.

You can visualize earth energy as being whatever color that is comfortable for you- though often people use a green or brown for earth energy. If you tell yourself to bring up 15% earth energy you will get 15%. If you tell yourself you want 14% or 16% you will get what you ask for respectively. Your spiritual self can measure exactly! Please do not use more than 15%. Earth energy is very powerful and you only need enough to give yourself a sense of being grounded. This earth energy will give you solidity and strength. It will also clean out your leg channels. When you conceive of a project or activity it is your legs that take the energy and manifest or act upon your ideas.

As you run energy through your legs you are cleaning the channels so there is more instant communication between your WILL and your ACTIVITY.

At the top of your head is an energy center called your Crown Chakra. It also opens and closes like the iris of an eye or the lens of a camera. Be aware of your Crown Chakra (but keep your consciousness in the Center of Your Head) and open your Crown Chakra. Imagine your Crown Chakra opening up as a spiral to a place that is comfortable for you and allow about 85% soft golden cosmic energy to come down your Crown Chakra, along the back of your spine and into your First Chakra where it mixes with the earth energy coming up your legs. As they mix together the two energies have a natural reaction and form a pumping movement, which propels the mixture of energy up the front of your spine, and back out your head and your Crown Chakra where it fountains out into your aura. Some of the energy branches off and moves across your shoulders and down your arms and out the palms of your hands. Therefore, you really want to open up your hand chakras (like the iris of an eye it opens as a spiral) so that your energy can move easily through your palms. Also, some of the energy goes back down your legs and out your feet. Let any excess energy go down your grounding cord. Now keep this energy constantly running through you.

You can run energy for five or ten minutes at a time in the beginning. When you wish to stop running energy bend over and stretch and drop your head and arms toward the ground and let any excess energy from the top of your head and your shoulders run out into the ground. This process is called DUMPING ENERGY. Often when you Run Energy excess energy will collect at the top of your head or on your shoulders. It is easy to DUMP ENERGY after you finish Running Energy. Now sit back up in the chair, open your eyes and take a good look around and get your bearings. Running Energy is an altered state of consciousness and often you want to bring yourself back to "normal" for a minute when you have finished.

Running Energy allows you to raise the energy vibration of your body so that your Higher Being can communicate more easily through it. As you learn the meditation of Running Energy you might notice that many things in life seem simpler and easier to accomplish. Running Energy moves out other people's energy, ideas and concepts, which means that you have more space in your own energy field to use for your own perceptions. The energy running through your arms clears your healing and creative energy. The energy running through your legs enables you to put thought into motion and act upon your ideas.

You can use Running Energy as a daily meditation for five, ten or twenty or more minutes at the beginning or end of the day or just sit and Run Energy during the day to "clear" yourself. The Running Energy Meditation is the process of combining cosmic and earth energies. These neutral energies become your own essence as you allow them to run through your energy field. Miraculously, as you work with your spiritual energy you will begin to allow yourself to see as spirit sees; know what your spirit knows and feel energized, enlightened and at one with your inner self.

GROWTH PERIODS

If you Run Energy then you will begin to release old energy, old patterns, old fears and you will change- and the first part of that change is going into what we call a Growth Period. A growth period is when you let go of something and your aura turns bright spring green like a spring tree and you do not have your old information or pattern any more but you have not yet brought in any new information or way to do things.

While you are in a growth period there is some confusion, your grounding might be a little weaker and you are in a transition space. It is wise not to make any major decisions until your new information comes in and your aura turns another color. Once your new information comes in you have reached a higher vibration and you know what to do.

While in a growth period you want to validate your body-food, sex, hugs, massage and whatever makes you feel good. You do not want to take on any more transition growth until you have shifted past your growth period as too much growth at once can be debilitating.

Most growth periods are short lived - but once in a while you will have these spiritual growth periods that actually continue as a cycle for three life times but we do not worry about these as they are not so common and just happen. You will not notice these unless you are very psychic or really pay attention to your Past Lives.

A growth period can last one minute, half an hour, a day, a week, a month, a year, a lifetime or many lifetimes. Most growth periods last less than two weeks. Some people are aware of what a growth period feels like and how it affects you. Usually you get to recognize what a growth period feels like. Once you get through the growth period and bring in your new information you feel more capable and are ready to take new action in your life.

Often people think of growth as plateaus that we struggle to reach and then just stay there for eons. But it does not really work that way. We are always in a series of small growth periods, like climbing in the hill country, and occasionally we climb the mountain and reach a higher plateau but just as you get comfortable and feel acclimated to your new plateau—your new self-- you will usually go into a new growth period! If you do psychic work, spiritual energetic healing, or clairvoyant or intuitive work of any kind, you will go into constant growth periods. Usually the first two years of doing this type of energetic work will cause you to have great and grand growth periods that shift your entire physical, emotional, mental and spiritual energetic bodies. After that, you will usually have mastered the ups and downs of a growth period and you will not react so intensely to your growth.

RUNNING ENERGY DAILY

When you Run Energy regularly you enable yourself to clean every cell, energy channel, energy center (chakra) in your body. Your aura gets light and bright. Your eyes get clear. Your skin improves. You might even seem to have a glow about you. Of course I am speaking about a person who Runs Energy between one and two hours a day—every day. Most students of clairvoyant healing start Running Energy for 10 minutes a day and then build up to about 45 minutes or one hour a day of Running Energy. Clairvoyants who work professionally Run Energy while they are doing Readings, and also Run Energy for two hours a day. But that usually takes a year or two to build up to it. It is like building up your intuitive muscles.

Running Energy gives you permission to bring in higher information to your body. You start to know things that are intuitive or Inner Plane information. You remember your dreams, have visions that are truthful, and have interesting revelations.

Most people are unaware of the higher levels of information that pass through their consciousness and their bodies but once you start to ground and run energy you begin to be aware of it. We call this state of constant awareness, "conscious awareness." Running Energy is an altered state of consciousness that is a light trance state. By Running Energy for twenty to thirty minutes a day you can clean out your entire system - the chakras and the aura - without any effort.

You always want to be awake and aware when you run energy‑ if you go to sleep or go out of your body it does not work. Running Energy is an "in the body" meditation. You should find that after a few weeks you will have a great deal of energy, which is why we call Running Energy an "energizing meditation."

RUNNING ENERGY IS A VERY SAFE METHOD OF OPENING THE SYSTEM AS LONG AS YOU ARE AWARE OF AND USE THESE METHODS:

Always Run Energy in a safe place where you feel comfortable since it "opens" you up, and always Run Energy while you are sitting in a chair with your feet firmly planted on the ground so that you are grounded. You want to finish Running Energy by sending your excess energy flow into the ground. This is so that you can distinctly come out of the trance state and back to your normal awareness.

If you follow these basic guidelines you will find that Running Energy is a very powerful energizing means of opening up to your internal self as well as your Higher Being and the natural Cosmic Oneness of the Universe that we are all a part of.

De-Energizing Mental Image
Pictures or commonly called
Blowing something up

Now that you are Grounded and in the Center of Your Head you can begin to use the Clearsight skill of transforming static or stuck energy patterns. This is a skill you can use all day long in daily life.

(It is best to learn this exercise while you are sitting in a chair, Grounded, in the Center of your Head and Running Energy with your eyes closed.) Once you know how to use this skill well you can use it during a healing or anytime during the day when it is useful.

This is a process of exploring the world of creation and destruction, the constant interchange of the energy flow on this planet. First of all, you create something. So right out in front of you, in front of and outside of your energy field create a big box.

Look at your box. If you can see your box then you are being a clairvoyant, a person who can see energy and images. Then create a stick of dynamite under your box and blow up your box into tiny little particles of energy. Send everyone else's energy back to them. Just give it a push and say "go home" and it will go back to wherever it originally came from. And bring all of your energy back to you as a golden sun above your head and let it come in and fill up your aura and own it.

Your ability to create something is a wonderful gift. But you also have the ability to destroy that energy because you know that you can create it again, and probably even better the second time around. Creation and destruction is a general feature of this planet.

What we create we can destroy because we can create it once more. Creating the box and destroying it is like taking a kernel of corn and making popcorn, or a glass of water and making ice cubes, or a raw egg and making a fried egg. It is taking our ability to change or transform energy.

Very often we find patterns stuck in our energy field: old belief systems, old ways of doing things, or old patterns in relationships that hold us back. These old energy patterns happen when we store our energy in a fixed form. We can release this energy and let go of our old pattern by simply allowing ourselves to blow up our old pattern. Once we have released the energy in our old pattern we can bring the energy it once was back to us as new life force energy and have more energy literally to explore our life experience with.

You can put anything in a box and blow it up and get the energy out of it. You can blow up bad feelings, jealousy, physical and emotional pain, and anxiety. You can even blow up another person. It will not hurt the person. It will simply send the energy of that person that is in your aura back to them. The only thing you should not blow up is any part of your own body. This would invalidate your body. If you want to get rid of fat or pain in your body simply take just the fat or the pain and blow it up. But if you do not like some part of your body do not blow it up. Simply blow up what you do not like but not your actual body. In this way you can release pain, old unneeded emotion, bad self esteem and fear. If you have a special song or a special food connected to an old relationship blow it up so you can move on to your next true love.

You can blow up boxes all day long! Whenever someone says something to you that causes you to react you just immediately on the spot put it in a rose and blow it up. As you use this skill on a daily basis you will find that you become more neutral in your dealings with people. When someone says something to you that you perceive as an insult you will be able to blow it up and then be neutral enough to see why that person REALLY uttered that statement.

To often we concentrate on the negative, on what we do not want, on what we do not like. Often if you ask someone what he or she wants in life, he will tell you what he does not want. You get what you put your energy into. If you feed the negative, the doubts, fears and dislikes then that is what your energy is tied up in. If you put these emotions in a box and blow them up and release them then you can go on to put the positive reality in front of you and create what you really want in life.

Most people store charged energy or emotion in their memories. When you perceive someone's aura you can see little units of energy, which clairvoyants call pictures. It is like watching a movie but stopping the projector and seeing individual frames or pictures. Each one of these pictures stores our information about a particular situation or memory. And usually each one of these pictures holds a great deal of emotion or charged energy. When we use this information or picture we become the effect of the charge in it.

If someone speaks to you of his childhood and you remember when you fell off of your bicycle and skinned your knee you are lighting up or becoming aware of your picture of your bicycle accident. This bicycle accident picture holds a charge of energy in it and if it is powerful enough it could cause your knee to hurt now, many years later. By removing the energy, or charge, from this incident you remove the hurt and the pain but you still have the memory. However once the energy is removed there is no energy charge to the memory. It is just a plain old memory that cannot hurt you anymore!

Many people block their memories because they cannot deal with the hurt and pain of the charged emotion in them. You can release these emotions by simply putting the memory or situation in a box and blowing it up. You do not even have to know why you feel sad, confused or hurt.

The stored or charged emotions that we hold onto can cause us to hold onto excess weight; old addictions, such as smoking, bad self image or self destructive behavior, and anti-success patterns. By placing these feelings or programs into a box we can begin to let go of them.

Often we will not let go of old or bad feelings because we do not want to look at them. We do not want to feel badly about ourselves or have to re-experience some old catastrophic event of our lives. With this system you do not have to re-experience any pain or bad feeling from the past. All you have to do is recognize that it exists and put it out in a box and blow it up. You do not have to stare at it, re-experience it or even understand it! You just have to acknowledge that a problem exists that blocks your happiness and well being and take it out of your energy field, put it in a box and blow it up as much as possible. This is one of the most simple and yet most powerful techniques on the planet if you use it consistently!

These skills will work for you if you use them. It does not matter whether you understand them as long as you practice them enough to affect some change in your energy field.

By blowing up boxes, by using this one simple technique you can clear out Karma and energy from your Past Lives, clean up the terror, fear and stuck emotion from your birth and your childhood, clear up the patterns you use to relate and love with and put yourself on the fast track to clarity with your purpose or goal in life.

THE CHAKRAS

Chakra is a Sanskrit word. In Sanskrit it has many meanings. As clairvoyants we tend to use two simple meanings. A chakra is an energy center that governs and controls your energy. It is your energy machinery. Chakras are vortexes of energy that send energy and information out to the world and receive energy and information for you. They open and close like a spiral. Each Chakra has a special ability that it governs. Whether or not you are aware of the chakras or understand them, they automatically function as your energy machinery that governs your body.

First Chakra

The First Chakra is located at the base of the spine in men and a little further forward between the ovaries in women. It is also called the Root Chakra since it is at the base or root of the body. The First Chakra governs your survival (food, clothing, and shelter) and your connection with earth energy. The First Chakra also governs your genetic material that is provided for procreation and childbirth.

Second chakra

The Second Chakra is located in the center of the abdomen, two finger lengths below your belly button. Your Second Chakra is called the "I feel" chakra and governs emotions, sensuality and sexuality. While the First Chakra governs your genetic procreation your Second Chakra governs your sexuality and sensuality in action. Whenever you say, "I feel," you are speaking from your Second Chakra.

Third chakra

Your Third Chakra is located at your solar plexus. The Third Chakra governs your ability to put thought into action. Your Third Chakra is the energy machinery that governs how much energy you have in your body and how you use it. The type of work you do; your hobbies; what you do on vacation; and what you do with your time; are all governed by your Third Chakra. The Third Chakra governs how you take your Will Power and make things happen or work for you.

Silver Cord

The Silver Cord is an energy cord that attaches from your Third Chakra to your Astral Body. It looks like a thin silvery cord. This cord can stretch for miles! It exists to tell you that you have a physical body and that after you travel astrally or spend your time out at nighttime you must come back to your physical body in this dimension on this planet. It is your reminder that you do indeed have a physical body. If this cord gets cut then you do not have a physical body. When you die this cord releases.

The Gear System

There is a gear system located within the Third Chakra. This gear system governs your metabolism by setting how slow or fast your energy vibrates.

Fourth chakra

Your Fourth Chakra, the Heart Chakra, is located at your breastbone. It governs your ability to be at one with the universe, your ability to love yourself and others and your self-identity and self esteem. The Heart Chakra is seen as the gateway to the body. From the Heart Chakra down are your body chakras. From the Fifth Chakra up are your spiritual chakras.

Upper Chakras: The Spiritual Chakras

Fifth chakra

Your Throat Chakra governs all forms of verbal and energy communication. There are specific types of abilities that exist within the Fifth Chakra. You have the ability to communicate telepathically with one person or with many people. You have the ability to use your Inner Voice to communicate with your body or to have your Higher Self communicate with your everyday consciousness. You also have the ability to be precognitive which is the ability to foretell the future. And you have the ability to be clairaudient- to hear Beings not in bodies and to hear people speak clairaudiently- which is non-verbally. Clair means clear and audient means to hear. All of these functions are located within the Throat Chakra.

Sixth chakra

Your sixth chakra is located in the center of your forehead. It governs how you see things; your ability to envision your past, present and future clairvoyantly. The machinery in the sixth chakra is like a camera that has a projection machine that sends a picture onto a screen located about a foot in front of your sixth chakra. If you sit back in the Center of your Head and just look at your screen you can see whatever you are interested in.

By using your Sixth Chakra you get in touch with your spirituality and can see the secrets of the universe and the knowledge of how spirit is eternal. All secrets are revealed by inner sight, the art of clairvoyancy. Since the Sixth Chakra is the highest chakra in the body it is the highest level of pure truthful knowledge you can access easily and consciously.

Seventh chakra—the crown chakra

Your Crown Chakra is located sitting on your head like a little crown. It is the seventh chakra and it is different from your lower chakras because the wide part of the wheel vortex sits on your head and it spirals upward from there.

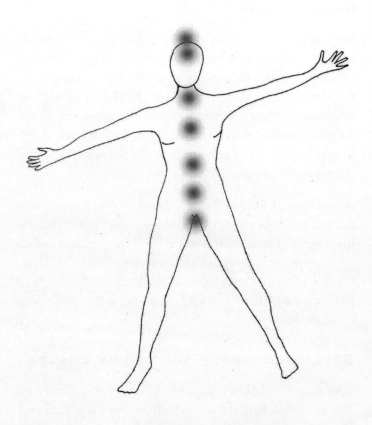

EVOLVING YOUR CONSCIOUS SELF

Why would you bother learning to see an aura? Because
by seeing the aura you get a tremendous amount of
fascinating useful information that also evolves you into
a higher level of awareness. By seeing the aura you can
see the truth of what happened in the past lives that you
view. You can understand the motivations of people.
You can come to understand a level of compassion and

truth from watching the true nature of a person. You learn to see the true inner person instead of viewing just the physical outward manifestation of a person's manner. And you can come to understand your true inner self, the part of you that takes bodies life after life and the part of you that is the true decision maker in all lives!

INTERPRETING WHAT YOU SEE

Sometimes when people first see an aura they see a white shimmering band of light around a person. If you see this it means you are just starting to open up to your ability to see the aura. Eventually you will see the aura in color. When you do see colors or images in the aura you have to know what it means to the person you are looking at. What bright green means to you might be different than what bright green means to the person you are viewing. It is easy to "see" the aura but takes practice, time, and experience to understand what you are seeing and what it means to the person you are viewing. Sometimes it is obvious what a color or picture means, depending on what layer of the aura it is in or just what it seems to say to you. Other times it is difficult to understand. If you see something and do not understand what it means simply explain exactly what you see in as neutral a way as possible to the person you are viewing. Often that person will understand what it means since it is their energy.

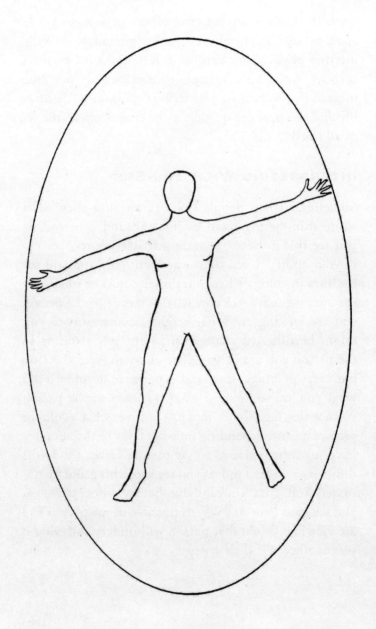

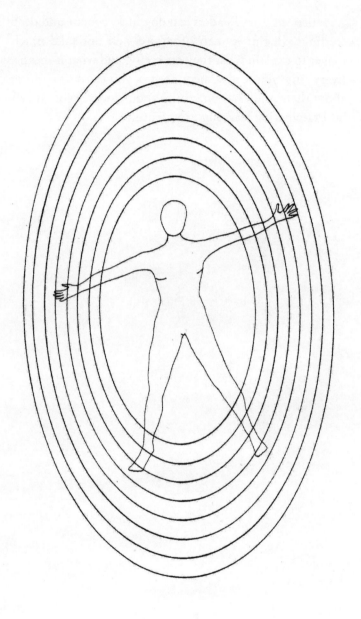

Experienced Aura Readers can do quick, concise and deep readings. Beginners can often see well but take much longer to explain what they are seeing and what it means. Every time you read someone's aura you learn something about them and also something about yourself too. It can be a fascinating learning experience.

About The Author

Levanah Shell Bdolak, the author of this book has been leading seminars in consciousness transformation skills since 1972 and travels nationally and internationally showing people how to shift their consciousness in easy practical ways. She shares these and other skills with executives and housewives in Tokyo every month at the Clearsight Japan Center and has taught internationally in Japan, France, England, Hong Kong, Thailand and nationally throughout the United States. She has shared clairvoyant and healing skills with doctors, nurses, physicists, therapists, masseuses, artists, executives, chefs, entertainers and housewives. Levanah is a professional clairvoyant, a motivational speaker, and a founder of the Clearsight Center in Santa Monica, CA, existing since April of 1980, where seminars are offered in a wide variety of subjects.

To reach Levanah or to get more information about the Clearsight Center and its programs:

www.clearsightaura.com

310-395-1170

Printed in Great Britain
by Amazon.co.uk, Ltd.,
Marston Gate.